On Evil

TERRY EAGLETON

On Evil

YALE UNIVERSITY PRESS
New Haven and London

Published with assistance from the foundation
established in memory of Philip Hamilton McMillan of
the Class of 1894, Yale College.

Set in Adobe type by Keystone Typesetting, Inc.
Printed in the United States of America.

Library of Congress Cataloging-in-Publication Data
Eagleton, Terry, 1943–

On evil / Terry Eagleton.
p.   cm.
Includes bibliographical references and index.
ISBN 978-0-300-15106-0 (hardcover : alk. paper)
1. Good and evil. I. Title.
BJ1401.E23 2010
111′.84—dc22
2009040138

A catalogue record for this book is available
from the British Library.

This paper meets the requirements of
ANSI/NISO Z39.48-1992 (Permanence of Paper).

10 9 8 7 6 5 4 3 2 1

To Henry Kissinger

Contents

On Evil

INTRODUCTION

Fifteen years ago, two ten-year-old boys tortured and killed a toddler in the north of England. There was an outcry of public horror, though why the public found this particular murder especially shocking is not entirely clear. Children, after all, are only semi-socialised creatures who can be expected to behave pretty savagely from time to time. If Freud is to be credited, they have a weaker superego or moral sense than their elders. In this sense, it is surprising that such grisly events do not occur more often. Perhaps children murder each other all the time and are simply keeping quiet about it. William Golding, an author whose work we shall be considering in a moment, seems to believe in his novel *Lord of the Flies* that a bunch of unsupervised schoolboys on a desert island would slaughter each other before the week was out.

Perhaps this is because we are ready to believe all kinds of sinister things about children, since they seem like a half-alien race in our midst. Since they do not work, it is not clear what they are for. They do not have sex, though perhaps they are keeping quiet about this too. They have the uncanniness of things which resemble us in some ways but not in others. It is not hard to fantasise that they are collectively conspiring against us, in the manner of John Wyndham's fable *The Midwich Cuckoos*. Because children are not fully part of the social game, they can be seen as innocent; but for just the same reason they can be regarded as the spawn of Satan. The Victorians swung constantly between angelic and demonic views of their offspring.

A police officer involved in the case of the murdered toddler declared that the moment he clapped eyes on one of the culprits, he knew that he was evil. This is the kind of thing that gives evil a bad name. The point of literally demonising the boy in this way was to wrong-foot the softhearted liberals. It was a preemptive strike against those who might appeal to social conditions in seeking to understand why they did what they did. And such understanding can always bring forgiveness in its wake. Calling the action evil meant that it was beyond comprehension. Evil is unintelligible. It is just a thing in itself, like boarding a crowded commuter train wearing only a giant boa constrictor. There is no context which would make it explicable.

Sherlock Holmes's great antagonist, the fiendishly evil Professor Moriarty, is presented as almost entirely without such a context. Yet it is significant that Moriarty is an Irish name, and Conan Doyle was writing at a time when there was much anxiety about revolutionary Irish Fenianism in Britain. Perhaps the Fenians reminded Doyle of his own drunken, violent Irish father, who had been locked away in a lunatic asylum. Making someone called Moriarty an image of pure evil is thus probably more explicable than it appears. Even so, evil is still often supposed to be without rhyme or reason. An English Evangelical bishop wrote in 1991 that clear signs of Satanic possession included inappropriate laughter, inexplicable knowledge, a false smile, Scottish ancestry, relatives who have been coal miners, and the habitual choice of black for dress or car colour. None of this makes sense, but then that is how it is with evil. The less sense it makes, the more evil it is. Evil has no relations to anything beyond itself, such as a cause.

In fact, the word has come to mean, among other things, "without a cause." If the child killers did what they did because of boredom or bad housing or parental neglect, then (so the police officer may have feared) what they did was forced upon them by their circumstances; and it followed that they could not be punished for it as severely as he might have wished. This mistakenly implies that an action which has a cause cannot be freely undertaken. Causes in this view are forms of coercion. If our actions have causes, we are not responsible for them. I cannot be responsible for staving in your skull with a candlestick, since it was your reproving tap on my cheek that caused it. Evil, on the other hand, is thought to be uncaused, or to be its own cause. This, as we shall see, is one of its several points of resemblance with good. Apart from evil, only God is said to be the cause of himself.

There is a kind of tautology or circular argument implicit in the policeman's view. People do evil things because they are evil. Some people are evil in the way that some things are coloured indigo. They commit their evil deeds not to achieve some goal, but just because of the sort of people they are. But might this not mean that they can't help doing what they do? For the policeman, the idea of evil is an alternative to such determinism. But it seems that we have thrown out a determinism of environment only to replace it with one of character. It is now your character, not your social conditions, which drives you to unspeakable deeds. And though it is easy enough to imagine an environment being changed—slums demolished, youth clubs set up, crack dealers driven out—it is harder to imagine such a total transformation when it comes to the question of human character. How could I be totally transformed and still be me? Yet if I happen to be evil, only such a deep-seated change will do.

So people like the policeman are really pessimists, even though they would probably bristle at the accusation. If Satan is what you are up against, rather than adverse social conditions, evil would seem to be unbeatable. And this is depressing news for (among other people) the police. Calling the boys evil dramatises the gravity of their crime, and seeks to cut off tenderhearted appeals to social conditions. It makes the culprits harder to forgive. But it does so only at the cost of suggesting that this kind of malignant behaviour is here to stay.

If the young killers of the toddler could not help being evil, however, then the fact is that they were innocent. Most of us, to be sure, recognise that small children can no more be evil than get divorced or enter into purchase agreements. Yet there are always those who believe in bad blood or malevolent genes. If some people really are born evil, however, they are no more responsible for this condition than being born with cystic fibrosis. The condition which is supposed to damn them succeeds only in redeeming them. The same goes for regarding terrorists as psychotic, a term which the British government's top security adviser has used for them. One wonders whether this man is really up to his job. If terrorists really are mad, then they are ignorant of what they are doing and are therefore morally innocent. They should accordingly be nursed with tender care in psychiatric hospitals rather than have their genitals mutilated in secret Moroccan prisons.

Men and women who are evil are sometimes said to be "possessed." But if they really are the helpless victims of demonic powers they are to be pitied, not condemned. The film *The Exorcist* is interestingly ambiguous about whether we should feel loathing or compassion for its diabolical little heroine. People who are supposedly possessed raise the hoary old question of freedom and determinism in thrillingly theatrical form. Is the devil inside the *Exorcist* child the true essence of her being (in which case we should fear and loathe her), or is it an alien invader (in which case we should feel pity for her)? Is she just the defenceless puppet of this power, or does it spring straight from who she is? Or is evil a case of self-alienation, in the sense that this hideous force is both you and not you? Perhaps it is a kind of fifth columnist, yet one installed at the very core of your identity. In that case, we ought to feel pity and fear at the same time, as Aristotle thinks we should when watching tragedy.

Those who wish to punish others for their evil, then, need to claim that they are evil of their own free will. Perhaps they have deliberately chosen evil as their end, like Shakespeare's Richard III, with his defiant "I am determined to prove a villain"; the Satan of Milton's *Paradise Lost,* with his "Evil, be thou my good!"; or Jean-Paul Sartre's Goetz in the play *Lucifer and the Lord,* with his boast "I do Evil for Evil's sake." Yet you might always claim that people like these, who consciously opt for evil, must already be evil to do so. Maybe they are somehow opting for what they already are, like Sartre's waiter playing at being a waiter. Maybe they are simply coming out of the moral closet, rather than assuming an entirely new identity.

The policeman in the toddler killing case, so it would seem, was trying to discredit the liberal doctrine that to understand all is to forgive all. This might be taken to mean that people are indeed answerable for what they do, but that an awareness of their circumstances will incline us to treat them leniently. But it might also be taken to suggest that, if our actions are rationally explicable, we are not responsible for them. The truth, on the contrary, is that reason and freedom are bound closely together. For those who do not grasp this point, trying to account for wicked acts is always a devious attempt to let their perpetrators off the hook. But to explain why I spend my weekends cheerfully boiling badgers alive is not necessarily to condone what I do. Not many people imagine that historians seek to explain the rise of Hitler in order to make him look more alluring. For some commentators, trying to grasp what motivates Islamic suicide bombers by, say, pointing to the despair and devastation of the Gaza Strip, is to absolve them of their guilt. But you can condemn those who blow up little children in the name of Allah without assuming that there is no explanation for their outrageous behaviour— that they pulverise people simply for kicks. You do not have to believe that the explanation in question is sufficient reason to justify what they do. Hunger is a sufficient reason for smashing a bakery window at two o'clock in the morning, but it is not usually regarded as an acceptable one, at least not by the police. I am not, incidentally, suggesting that resolving the Israel-Palestine problem, or any other situation in which Muslims today feel abused and humiliated, would make Islamic terrorism disappear overnight. The grim truth is that it is probably too late for that. Like accumulating capital, terror-ism has a momentum of its own. But it is a fair bet that, without those humiliations, such terrorism would never have got off the ground.

It is also odd to assume that understanding is bound to lead to greater tolerance. In fact, the reverse is often true. The more we learn of the futile massacres of the First World War, for example, the less we feel they can be justified. Explanations may sharpen moral judgments as well as soften them. Besides, if evil really is beyond explanation—if it is an unfathomable mystery—how can we even know enough about it to condemn evildoers? The word "evil" is generally a way of bringing argu-ments to an end, like a fist in the solar plexus. Like the idea of taste, over which there is supposedly no arguing, it is an end-stopping kind of term, one which forbids the raising of further questions. Either human actions are explicable, in which case they cannot be evil; or they are evil, in which case there is nothing more to be said about them. The argument of this book is that neither of these viewpoints is true.

No Western politician today could afford to suggest in public that there are rational motivations behind the dreadful things that terrorists get up to. "Rational" might too easily be translated as "commendable." Yet there is nothing irrational about robbing a bank, even if it is not generally considered to be commendable. (Though as Bertolt Brecht remarked, "What's robbing a bank compared to founding one?"). The Irish Republican Army obviously had well-pondered political ends, however atrocious some of their methods of achieving them. Yet some in the British media still tried to portray them as psychopaths. If we are not to humanise these ogres, so the assumption goes, there must simply be no rhyme or reason in their actions. But it is precisely the fact that they are human that makes what terrorists do so appalling. If they really were inhuman, we might not be in the least surprised by their behaviour. The horrors they perpetrate might be everyday trifles on Alpha Centauri.

The police officer's use of the term "evil" was clearly ideological. He was probably afraid that people would go easy on the offenders because of their tender years, and saw the need to insist that even ten year olds are morally responsible agents. (In fact, the public did not go easy on them at all. There are still those who are eager to kill them now they have been released from custody.) So "evil" can be translated here as "answerable for one's own actions," just like its opposite, good. Goodness is also sometimes thought to be free of social conditioning. The greatest of modern philosophers, Immanuel Kant, held just such a view. This is why Dickens's Oliver Twist remains untainted by the low life of criminal London into which he is plunged. Oliver never loses his sweet countenance, moral rectitude, and mysterious ability to speak Standard English despite having been brought up in a workhouse. (The Artful Dodger, one suspects, would have spoken broad Cockney even if he had been raised in Windsor Castle.) But this is not because Oliver is a saint. If he is immune to the polluting influence of thieves, thugs, and prostitutes, it is less because he is morally superior than because his goodness is somehow genetic, as resistant to the mouldings of circumstance as freckles or sandy hair. If Oliver just can't help being good, however, his virtue is surely no more to be admired than the size of his ears. Besides, if it is his purity of will which renders him immune to the malignancy of the underworld, can the underworld really be as malignant as all that? Wouldn't a truly wicked Fagin succeed in corrupting that will? Doesn't the child's unassailable virtue unwittingly let the old rascal off the hook? We might also ask ourselves, with Oliver's impregnable innocence in mind, whether we really admire a goodness that cannot be put to the test. The old-fashioned puritan view that virtue must prove its credentials in strenuous combat with its enemies, and in doing so must expose itself to something of their depraved power, has something to be said for it.

As far as responsibility is concerned, Kant and a right-wing tabloid like the *Daily Mail* have a good deal in common. Morally speaking, both hold that we are entirely responsible for what we do. In fact, such self-responsibility is thought to be the very essence of morality. On this view, appeals to social conditioning are simply a cop-out. Many people, conservatives point out, grow up in dismal social conditions yet become law-abiding citizens. This is rather like arguing that because some smokers don't die of cancer, nobody who smokes dies of cancer. It is this doctrine of absolute self-responsibility which has helped to overpopulate the death rows of U. S. prisons. Human beings must be seen as wholly autonomous (literally: "a law unto themselves"), because to invoke the influence of social or psychological factors on what they do would be to reduce them to zombies. In the Cold War era, this was equivalent to reducing them to that worst horror of all: Soviet citizens. So killers with a mental age of five, or battered wives who finally turn on their pugnacious husbands, must be as guilty as Goebbels. Better a monster than a machine.

There is, however, no absolute distinction between being influenced and being free. A good many of the influences we undergo have to be interpreted in order to affect our behaviour; and interpretation is a creative affair. It is not so much the past that shapes us as the past as we (consciously or unconsciously) interpret it. And we can always come to decipher it differently. Besides, someone free of social influences would be just as much a nonperson as a zombie. In fact, he or she would not really be a human being at all. We can act as free agents only because we are shaped by a world in which this concept has meaning, and which allows us to act upon it. None of our distinctively human behaviour is free in the sense of being absolved from social determinants, which includes such distinctively human behaviour as poking people's eyes out. We would not be able to torture and massacre without having picked up a great many social skills. Even when we are alone, it is not in the sense in which a coal scuttle or the Golden Gate Bridge is alone. It is only because we are social animals, able through language to share our inner life with others, that we can speak of such things as autonomy and self-responsibility in the first place. They are not terms that apply to earwigs. To be responsible is not to be bereft of social influences, but to relate to such influences in a particular way. It is to be more than just a puppet of them. "Monster" in some ancient thought meant, among other things, a creature that was wholly independent of others.

Human beings can indeed achieve a degree of self-determination. But they can do so only in the context of a deeper dependence on others of their kind, a dependence which is what makes them human in the first place. It is this, as we shall see, that evil denies. Pure autonomy is a dream of evil. It is also *the* myth of middle-class society. (Which is not to say that to be middle class is to be evil. Not even the most militant of Marxists believe that, partly because they tend not to believe in evil in the first place.) In Shakespearian drama, those who claim to depend upon themselves alone, claiming sole authorship of their own being, are almost always villains. You can appeal to people's absolute moral autonomy, then, as a way of convicting them of evil; but in doing so you are pandering to a myth that the evil themselves have fallen for in a big way.

Decades before the two boys killed the toddler, another public outcry over the death of an infant shook Britain from end to end. This was the wave of moral hysteria over Edward Bond's play *Saved,* in which a group of teenagers stone a baby to death in its carriage. The scene is a fine illustration of the old cliché that just messing around can always get out of hand. Its purpose is to demonstrate, step by inexorable step, how a bunch of chronically bored young people could commit such an atrocity without being in the least wicked. The devil, as they say, makes work for idle hands, which rather oddly suggests that keeping yourself occupied is the best way to avoid landing up before a war crimes tribunal. The trouble with the wicked, however, is that they are far too busy, rather than not busy enough. We shall see later how evil has much to do with a sense of futility or meaninglessness; and one of the points of the Bond scene, heartless though it may sound, is that the teenagers are actually cobbling together some meaning for themselves. It was the ordinariness of the episode, quite as much as the horror of the act itself, which raised the hackles of the perpetually affrontable British public. We were being shown how the unspeakable can flow from the utterly familiar, which seemed to diminish the gravity of the action. Evil is supposed to be special, not commonplace. It is not like lighting up a cigarette. Malevolence cannot be monotonous. We shall see later how this, ironically, is a view shared by the evil themselves.

For there are indeed evil acts and individuals, which is where the softhearted liberals and the tough-minded Marxists alike are mistaken. As far as the latter go, the American Marxist Fredric Jameson writes of "the archaic categories of good and evil."[1] One is forced to assume that Jameson is not of the view that the victory of socialism would be a good thing. The

English Marxist Perry Anderson implies that terms like "good" and "evil" are relevant to individual conduct only—in which case it is hard to see why tackling famines, combating racism, or disarming nuclear missiles should be described as good.[2] Marxists do not need to reject the notion of evil, as my own case would exemplify; but Jameson and some of his leftist colleagues do so partly because they tend to confuse the moral with the moralistic. In this, ironically, they are at one with the likes of the U.S. Moral Majority. Moralism means regarding moral judgments as existing in a sealed domain of their own, quite distinct from more material matters. This is why some Marxists are uneasy with the whole idea of ethics. It sounds to them like a distraction from history and politics. But this is a misunderstanding. Properly understood, moral inquiry weighs all these factors together. This is as true of Aristotle's ethics as it is of Hegel's or Marx's. Moral thought is not an alternative to political thought. For Aristotle, it is part of it. Ethics considers questions of value, virtue, qualities, the nature of human conduct and the like, while politics attends to the institutions which allow such conduct to flourish or to be suppressed. There is no impassable gulf here between the private and the public. If morality is not just about the personal life, neither is politics just about the public one.

People differ on the question of evil. A recent poll reported that a belief in sin is highest in Northern Ireland (91 percent), and lowest in Denmark (29 percent). Nobody with any firsthand acquaintance with that pathologically religious entity known as Northern Ireland (the greater part of Ulster) will be in the least amazed by that first finding. Ulster Protestants clearly take a dimmer view of human existence than the hedonistic Danes. One takes it that Danes, like most other people who have been reading the newspapers, do indeed believe in the reality of greed, child pornography, police violence, and the barefaced lies of the pharmaceutical companies. It is just that they prefer not to call these things sins. This may be because they think of sin as an offence against God rather than as an offence against other people. It is not a distinction that the New Testament has much time for.

On the whole, postmodern cultures, despite their fascination with ghouls and vampires, have had little to say of evil. Perhaps this is because the postmodern man or woman— cool, provisional, laid-back and decentred—lacks the depth that true destructiveness requires. For postmodernism, there is nothing really to be redeemed. For high modernists like Franz Kafka, Samuel Beckett, or the early T. S. Eliot, there is indeed something to be redeemed, but it has become impossible to say quite what. The desolate, devastated landscapes of Beckett have the look of a world crying out for salvation. But salvation presupposes sinfulness, and Beckett's wasted, eviscerated human figures are too sunk in apathy and inertia even to be mildly immoral. They cannot even muster the strength to hang themselves, let alone set fire to a village of innocent civilians.

To acknowledge the reality of evil, however, is not necessarily to hold that it lies beyond all explanation. You can believe in evil without supposing that it is supernatural in origin. Ideas of evil do not have to posit a cloven-hoofed Satan. It is true that some liberals and humanists, along with the laid-back Danes, deny the existence of evil. This is largely because they regard the word "evil" as a device for demonising those who are really nothing more than socially unfortunate. It is what one might call the community-worker theory of morality. It is true that this is one of the word's most priggish uses, as we have seen already. But to reject the idea of evil for this reason works better if you are thinking of unemployed council-estate heroin addicts rather than serial killers or the Nazi SS. It is hard to see the SS as merely unfortunate. One should be careful not to let the Khmer Rouge off the same hook on which delinquent teenagers are impaled.

It is part of the argument of this book that evil is not fundamentally mysterious, even though it transcends everyday social conditioning. Evil as I see it is indeed metaphysical, in the sense that it takes up an attitude toward being as such, not just toward this or that bit of it. Fundamentally, it wants to annihilate the lot of it. But this is not to suggest that it is necessarily supernatural, or that it lacks all human causality. Many things—art and language, for example—are more than just a reflex of their social circumstances, but this is not to say that they drop from the skies. The same is true of human beings in general. If there is no necessary conflict between the historical and the transcendent, it is because history itself is a process of self-transcendence. The historical animal is one who is constantly able to go beyond itself. There are, so to speak, "horizontal" forms of transcendence as well as "vertical" ones. Why should we always think of the latter?

The modern age has witnessed what one might call a transition from the soul to the psyche. Or, if one prefers, from theology to psychoanalysis. There are many senses in which the latter is a stand-in for the former. Both are narratives of human desire—though for religious faith that desire can finally be consummated in the kingdom of God, whereas for psychoanalysis it must remain tragically unappeased. In this sense, psychoanalysis is the science of human discontent. But so, too, is theology. With Freud, repression and neurosis play the role of what Christians have traditionally known as original sin. In each case, human beings are seen as born in sickness. But they are thereby not beyond redemption. Happiness is not beyond our grasp; it is just that it requires of us a traumatic breaking down and remaking, for which the Christian term is conversion. Both sets of belief investigate phenomena which finally outstrip the bounds of human knowledge, whether you call this the enigmatic unconscious or an unfathomable God. Both are well supplied with rituals of initiation, confession, and excommunication, and both are ridden with internecine feuds. They are also alike in provoking derisive incredulity from the worldly, commonsensical, and hard-headed. The theory of evil I expound in this book draws heavily on the thought of Freud, not least on his idea of the death drive; but I hope in the process to show how this kind of argument remains faithful to many a traditional theological insight. One advantage of this approach is that it ranges more widely than most recent discussions of evil have done. A lot of these inquiries have been wary of straying too far from Kant, a philosopher who has much of great interest to say of evil, and from the Holocaust. In the end, evil is indeed all about death—but about the death of the evildoer as much as that of those he annihilates. To understand what this means, however, we need first to look at a few works of fiction.

CHAPTER ONE

Fictions of Evil

There aren't many novels in which the main character dies in the first few paragraphs. There are even fewer in which this is the only character in the book. We would be bemused if Jane Austen's Emma Woodhouse were to break her neck in the first chapter of *Emma,* or Henry Fielding's Tom Jones were to be stillborn in the novel's opening sentences. Something like this, however, is what happens in William Golding's novel *Pincher Martin,* which begins with a man drowning:

> He was struggling in every direction, he was the
> centre of the writhing and kicking knot of his own

body. There was no up or down, no light and no air. He felt his mouth open of itself and the shrieked word burst out.

"Help!"

Given that there is no help to hand, and that the man, Christopher Martin, is wallowing in the middle of the ocean, this promises to be a gratifyingly short novel. With commendable presence of mind, however, he manages to kick off his sea boots, inflate his lifebelt, and struggle his way to a nearby rock, where he survives for a while. Except that his efforts are really in vain. The truth is that Martin dies before he heaves his boots off, though he does not know it. Neither does the reader, who discovers this only in the novel's last line. In watching Martin scrambling around on his imaginary rock, we are privy to the condition of the living dead.

Pincher Martin is the tale of a man who refuses to die. Yet we soon learn from a series of flashbacks that this grasping, lecherous, manipulative naval officer was never really alive in the first place. "He was born," a colleague remarks, "with his mouth and flies open and both hands out to grab." His isolation on the rock magnifies the fact that he has been a solitary predator all along. Martin uses other people as instruments of his own profit or pleasure, and on the rock he is reduced to using his own exhausted body as a rusty piece of mechanism for accomplishing various tasks. As the sinewy, muscular style of the novel suggests, the hero is stripped down to his animal-ity—to the instinctively self-preservative creature he has always been. It is fitting, then, that he is dead without knowing it, since death reduces the body to a meaningless piece of matter. It represents the divorce of materiality and meaning.

Estranged from his own body, Martin squats inside it rather as a man might sit inside a crane, operating its limbs like so many levers. Evil involves a split between body and spirit—between an abstract will to dominate and destroy, and the meaningless piece of flesh that this will inhabits. Martin does not see but "uses" his eyes to look at the things around him. While he was alive, he negated the reality of other people's bodies, treating their flesh merely as a mechanical means to his own satisfaction. Now, in a neatly ironic reversal, he deals with his own body as though it were someone else's. His extreme fatigue, which means that he has to shift his limbs by sheer force of will, magnifies the way he has treated other human bodies all along. Certainly his own body is no part of his identity. It is at war with his selfhood, rather than the place where that selfhood is made flesh. All that is still stirring in him is a sublimely unquenchable will to survive, which drives on the lumbering machinery of his body like a despot. Because it transcends all natural constraints, this will represents a kind of infinity. As such, it is a secular version of the God against whom Martin will find himself pitted in a life-and-death struggle.

This shipwrecked sailor, then, is a mass of lifeless stuff pinned together only by a relentless drive. This drive is located in what the novel calls the "dark centre"—the eternally vigilant core of consciousness buried somewhere inside Martin's skull, which seems the only place where he is truly alive (though even this will turn out to be an illusion). This dark centre is the hero's monstrous ego, which is unable to reflect on itself. This can be understood in both a factual and a moral sense. Human consciousness cannot nip behind itself, since when we reflect on ourselves it is still we who are doing the reflecting. Our sense of the murky regions from which consciousness springs is itself an act of consciousness, and thus already remote from that realm. But neither can Pincher Martin know himself for what he is, in the sense of getting a fix on his own predatory nature. If he were able to do this, he might be able to repent, and so to die for real. As it is, he is stuck fast within his own skull. Even the rock, whose contours seem curiously familiar to him all along, turns out to be the exact shape of a missing tooth in his gum. He is literally living inside his own head. Hell is not other people, as Jean-Paul Sartre claimed. It is exactly the opposite. It is being stuck for all eternity with the most dreary, unspeakably monotonous company of all: oneself.

What the novel portrays, in the figure of its dead-but-won't-lie-down protagonist, is a chilling image of Enlightenment Man. It is, to be sure, a grossly one-sided portrait of that mighty current of human emancipation, as one might expect from a conservative Christian pessimist like Golding. But it captures with superb immediacy some of its less savoury aspects. Martin, as we have seen, is a rationalist who treats the world, including his own and others' bodies, as mere valueless stuff to be moulded by his imperious will. All that counts is his own brutal self-interest. As a kind of latter-day colonialist Crusoe, he even seeks to exercise dominion over the rock on which he is marooned, giving names to its various sectors and manhandling its bits and pieces into some kind of order. It is almost as though his briskly efficient activity on the rock is a way of concealing from himself the fact that he is dead. In this sense, too, Martin behaves rather like Robinson Crusoe, who chops wood and builds stockades on his desert island with all the stolid common sense of a Home Counties carpenter. There is something reassuring about witnessing such stout Anglo-Saxon practicality even in the most exotic of settings. There is also something mildly insane about it.

In fact, it is practical intelligence that Martin values most highly. Deludedly, he sees himself as Prometheus, a mighty hero of the Enlightenment and Karl Marx's favourite mythological figure. Prometheus, too, was chained to a rock but refused to submit to the gods. "Give up, leave go" is the temptation seductively murmured in his ear; but he is terrified of slackening his grip on himself, which is what dying would involve. Since all he has ever had is himself, the only alternative to survival would be pure nothingness. And even his tormented half-life on the rock is preferable to no existence whatsoever.

Martin cannot die because he regards himself as too

precious to disappear forever. But he is also unable to die because he is incapable of love. Only the good are capable of dying. Martin cannot yield himself up to death because he has never been able to yield himself up to others in life. In this sense, how you die is determined by how you live. Death is a form of self-dispossession which must be rehearsed in life if it is to be successfully accomplished. Otherwise it will prove to be a cul-de-sac rather than a horizon. Being-for-others and being-toward-death are aspects of the same condition. *Pincher Martin* is sometimes taken to be a novel about hell, but it is really a story about purgatory. Purgatory is not an ante-room in which morally mediocre types sit around performing various degrading penances until their number is called and they shuffle shamefacedly forward into paradise. For Christian theology, it is the moment of death itself, when you discover whether you have enough love inside you to be able to give yourself away with only a tolerable amount of struggle. This is why martyrs—those who actively embrace their deaths in the service of others—traditionally go straight to heaven.

Martin is not in hell. Though he is dead on his feet, some ghostly trace of him still lingers on; and there can be no life in hell, which is a state of pure annihilation. There could no more be anyone "in" hell than there could be anyone in a material location called debt or love or despair. For traditional theology, to be in hell is to fall out of the hands of God by deliberately spurning his love, if such a condition is actually thinkable. In this sense, hell is the most florid compliment to human freedom one could imagine. If one can even reject the blandishments of one's Creator, one must be powerful indeed. But since there can be no life outside God, who is the source of all vitality, the finality of hell is a matter of extinction, not perpetuity. If there is such a thing as hellfire, it could only be the fire of God's ruthless love, which burns up those who cannot bear it. The damned are those who experience God as a Satanic terror, since he threatens to prise their selves apart. His love and mercy loosen their hold on themselves, and in doing so risk depriving them of their most precious possession. Those who live in fear of hellfire, then, can rest assured. The good news is that they will not roast for ever and ever. This is because the bad news is that they will simply be consumed to nothing.

This, in the end, is probably what happens to Christopher Martin, though we can't be sure. His friend Nathaniel, whose gauche, gangly innocence infuriates him rather as the sheer fact of Othello's existence irritates Iago beyond endurance, speaks to him of "the technique of dying into heaven," dissolving into the ultimate truth of things. Martin reacts rather less high-mindedly by trying to murder him. In our present warped condition, Nat argues, the love of God would appear to us as "sheer negation. Without form or void. You see? A sort of black lightning destroying everything we call life." God is a kind of sublime nothingness. He is a terrorist of love, whose implacable forgiveness is bound to seem like an intolerable affront to those who cannot let go of themselves. The damned are those who experience the "good" infinity of God as a "bad" one. In the same way, one can experience what art historians call the sublime (towering mountains, storms at sea, infinite skies) as either terrible or magnificent, or both.

Like Faust, the damned are too proud to submit to limit. They will not bow the knee to the finite, least of all to their own creatureliness. This is why pride is the characteristic Satanic vice. This is also why they are so terrified of death, which is the absolute limit of the human. The "good" nothing of God is counterpointed in the novel by the "bad" nothingness of Martin himself, his sheer incapacity for life. "I spit on your compassion . . . I shit on your heaven!" he snarls in the final showdown. As the lines of black lightning play mercilessly around him, probing for some crevice or point of weakness where they may penetrate, Martin is reduced to a pair of enormous lobster-like claws, locked like a protective carapace over the elusive dark centre of his selfhood. The lightning probes away at the claws, seeking with infinite patience to undo them:

> There was nothing but the centre and the claws. They were huge and strong and inflamed to red. They closed on each other. They contracted. They were outlined like a night sign against the absolute nothingness and they gripped their whole strength against each other . . . The lightning crept in. The centre was unaware of anything but the claws and

the threat . . . Some of the [lightning's] lines pointed to the centre, waiting for the moment when they could pierce it. Others lay against the claws, playing over them, prying for a weakness, wearing them away in a compassion that was timeless and without mercy.

And this is where we take leave of our hero. We do not learn whether the black lightning succeeds in its probing and prying. Perhaps Martin is not annihilated after all. We do not know whether the lightning of God's remorseless love turns out in his case to be a bad negativity or a good one—whether it obliterates him or transforms him. This is one reason why *Pincher Martin* is not a novel about hell.

There is a final point to note about the book's terrifyingly apocalyptic conclusion. When the black lightning begins its destructively re-creative work, the rock and the ocean are revealed to be mere paper fictions:

The sea stopped moving, froze, became paper, painted paper that was torn by a black line. The rock was painted on the same paper. The whole of the painted sea was tilted but nothing ran downhill into the black crack which had opened in it. The crack was utter, was absolute, was three times real . . . The lines of absolute blackness fell forward into the rock and it was proved to be as insubstan-

tial as the painted water. Pieces went and there was
no more than an island of papery stuff around the
claws and everywhere else there was the mode that
the centre knew as nothing.

Martin's self-created world turns out to be quite literally a
hollow fiction. It is no more than a fantasy designed to plug
the intolerable negativity of death. This final revelation is
particularly shocking given the novel's intensely physical style,
which works overtime to re-create the sensuous feel of things.
If anything has the air of reality, it is this jagged wedge of rock
and its frozen, skin-drenched tenant. Even this sense of solid-
ity, however, turns out to be an illusion. Evil may appear
robust and substantial, but it is in fact as flimsy as a spider's
web. There is another kind of negativity, however—that sym-
bolised by the black lightning of God's love—which is more
real than reality itself.

There may be some significance in Golding's choice of
surname for his hero. Not long before the novel's publication, a
book appeared describing Operation Mincemeat, a celebrated
ruse which took place toward the end of the Second World
War. British forces dropped a corpse dressed as a Royal Marines
officer off the coast of Spain, carrying letters which successfully
fooled the Germans about where the Allies planned to invade
Europe. The code name given to the corpse was William
Martin; and in the introduction to a new edition of an account
of the operation, Ewen Montagu's *The Man Who Never Was,*

John Julius Norwich raises the suggestion that the dead man, whose identity remains secret to this day, was one John McFarlane, a name which sounds Scottish.[1] In the film of Montagu's book, there are also one or two hints that the anonymous body is that of a Scot, possibly from the Hebrides. There is a reference to the Hebrides in *Pincher Martin,* which might just be an allusion to Martin's home. In Operation Mincemeat, a dead man saved thousands of the living, as the duped Germans diverted their troops from the Allies' true landing place. In Golding's novel, a dead man believes that he himself is rescued. But he was never really alive in the first place. Pincher Martin is the man who never was.

Several of Golding's novels are concerned with what is traditionally known as original sin. *Lord of the Flies,* for example, is a heavily loaded fable of the "darkness of men's hearts." The schoolboys' efforts to build a civilised order on their island are inevitably undermined by violence and sectarianism. I call the fable "heavily loaded" because it is easy to prove that civilisation is only skin-deep if the people you show trying to build it are only partly civilised animals in the first place (i.e., children). It is as easy as proving in the manner of George Orwell's novel *Animal Farm* that human beings cannot run their own affairs by portraying them as farmyard animals. In both cases, the form of the fable determines the moral outcome.

Another of Golding's novels, *The Inheritors,* actually pinpoints the moment of the Fall itself, as one "unfallen" tribe of early hominids encounters another, more dangerous and destructive culture. This second tribe, because of its greater capacity for language, has made the crucial transition to conceptual abstraction and technology. And this involves developing more deadly weapons. It is as though this more evolved community has cut its bonds with Nature and entered upon the precariousness of history proper, with all its ambiguous gains and losses. The Fall, with impeccable theological correctness, is thus portrayed as a fall up rather than down. It is a *felix culpa,* or fortunate fault, in which human beings "lapse" upward from the natural world and the innocence of the beasts into an exhilarating, sickeningly unstable history. It is, to adopt the title of another of Golding's novels, a free Fall—one bound up with the fatal, double-edged freedom which advanced linguistic consciousness brings in its wake.

Free Fall is the title of Golding's most subtle investigation of original sin, a condition which has nothing to do with slimy reptiles and forbidden fruit. "Original" here means "at the root," not "in the beginning." The novel perceives that being "fallen" has to do with the misery and exploitation that human freedom inevitably brings in its wake. It lies in the fact that we are self-contradictory animals, since our creative and destructive powers spring from much the same source. The philosopher Hegel considered that evil flourished the more individual freedom did. A creature equipped with language can develop far beyond the restricted scope of nonlinguistic creatures. It acquires godlike powers of creation. But like most potent sources of invention, these capabilities are also deeply dangerous. Such an animal is in constant peril of developing too fast, overreaching itself and bringing itself to nothing. There is something potentially self-thwarting or self-undoing about humanity. And this is what the biblical myth of the Fall is struggling to formulate, as Adam and Eve use their creative powers to undo themselves. Man is Faustian Man, too voraciously ambitious for his own well-being, perpetually driven beyond his own limits by the lure of the infinite. This creature cold-shoulders all finite things in his hubristic love affair with the illimitable. And since infinity is a kind of nothingness, the desire for this nothingness is an expression of what we shall see later as the Freudian death drive.

The Faustian fantasy, then, betrays a puritanical distaste for the fleshly. To achieve the infinite (a project known among other things as the American Dream), we would need to leap out of our wretchedly disabling bodies. What distinguishes capitalism from other historical forms of life is that it plugs directly into the unstable, self-contradictory nature of the human species. The infinite—the unending drive for profit, the ceaseless march of technological progress, the ever-expanding power of capital—is always at risk of crushing and overshooting the finite. Exchange-value, which as Aristotle recognised is potentially limitless, holds sway over use-value. Capitalism is a system which needs to be in perpetual motion simply to stay on the spot. Constant transgression is of its essence. No other historical system reveals so starkly the way in which potentially beneficent human powers are so easily perverted to baneful ends. Capitalism is not the cause of our "fallen" state, as the more naive kind of left-winger tends to imagine. But of all human regimes, it is the one which most exacerbates the contradictions built into a linguistic animal.

Thomas Aquinas taught that our reasoning is closely bound up with our bodies. Roughly speaking, we think the way we do because of the kind of animals we are. It belongs to our reasoning, for example, that it always goes on within a specific situation. We think from inside a particular perspective on the world. This is not an obstacle to grasping the truth. On the contrary, it is the only way we can grasp it. The only truths we can attain to are those appropriate to finite beings like ourselves. And these are the truths of neither angels nor anteaters. Overreachers, however, refuse to accept these enabling constraints. For them, only truths which are free of all perspective can be authentic. The only valid viewpoint is the God's-eye viewpoint. But this is a vantage point from which we humans would see nothing at all. For us, absolute knowledge would be utter blindness. Those who try to leap out of their finite situations in order to see more clearly end up seeing nothing at all. Those who aspire to be gods, like Adam and Eve, destroy themselves and end up lower than the beasts, who are not so plagued by sexual guilt that they need a fig leaf. Even so, this aberration is an essential part of our nature. It is a permanent possibility for rational animals like ourselves. We cannot think without abstraction, which involves reaching beyond the immediate. When abstract concepts allow us to incinerate whole cities, we know we have reached too far. A perpetual possibility of going awry is built into our capacity for sense-making. Without this possibility, reason could not function.

There is another sense in which freedom and destructiveness are bound up together. In the complex web of human destinies, where so many lives are meshed intricately together, the freely chosen actions of one individual may breed damaging, entirely unforeseeable effects in the lives of countless anonymous others. They may also return in alien form to plague ourselves. Acts that we and others have performed freely in the past may merge into an opaque process which appears without an author, confronting us in the present with all the intractable force of fate. In this sense, we are the creatures of our own deeds. A certain inescapable self-estrangement is thus built into our condition. "Freedom," observes Adrian Leverkühn in Thomas Mann's novel *Doctor Faustus,* "always inclines to dialectic reversals." This is why original sin is traditionally about an act of freedom (eating an apple), yet is at the same time a condition we did not choose, and one which is nobody's fault. It is "sin" because it involves guilt and injury, but not "sin" in the sense of willful wrong. Like desire for Freud, it is less a conscious act than a communal medium into which we are born.

The interwovenness of our lives is the source of our solidarity. But it also lies at the root of our mutual harm. As the philosopher Emmanuel Levinas writes, it is "as if persecution by the Other were at the basis of solidarity with the Other."[2] In a poignant moment in James Joyce's novel *Ulysses,* the long-suffering Jewish hero Leopold Bloom speaks up for love as the opposite of hate. It would be agreeable if this were true. But there are sound Freudian reasons for regarding love as deeply bound up with resentment and aggression. It may not be true, as Oscar Wilde claimed, that we always kill the thing we love, but it is certainly true that we tend to feel profoundly ambivalent about it. Given that love is a laborious process which requires a perilous risking of ourselves, this is scarcely surprising. The novelist Thomas Hardy knew that by a series of decisions which are both free and considerate of others, we can end up painting ourselves into corners where we cannot move an inch in any direction without inflicting grievous damage on those around us.

"People don't seem to be able to move without killing each other," remarks Sammy Mountjoy in Golding's *Free Fall.* It is only a short step from this to the feeling that simply to exist is to be guilty. It is this feeling that the doctrine of original sin is supposed to register. "Guilt reproduces itself in each of us," writes Theodor Adorno. "If we . . . knew at every moment what has happened and to what concatenations we owe our own existence, and how our own existence is interwoven with calamity, even if we have done nothing wrong . . . if one were fully aware of all things at every moment, one would really be unable to live."[3] To be implicated in a calamity without having done wrong: this is the very essence of original sin, as Adorno perceives. It is closely related to what tragic art traditionally sees as the "guilty innocent" figure of the scapegoat, who takes on the burden of others' misdeeds precisely because he is blameless himself.

This is what is so absurd about the Roman Catholic doctrine of the Immaculate Conception, according to which Jesus's mother, Mary, was conceived without original sin. It regards original sin as a kind of genetic stain which you might be fortunate enough to be born without, rather as you might be unfortunate enough to be born without a liver. Original sin, however, is not about being born either saintly or wicked. It is about the fact of being born in the first place. Birth is the moment when, without anyone having had the decency to consult us on the matter, we enter into a preexistent web of needs, interests, and desires—an inextricable tangle to which the mere brute fact of our existence will contribute, and which will shape our identity to the core. This is why babies in most Christian churches are baptised at birth, long before they know about sin or indeed about anything else. They have already drastically reordered the universe without being aware of it. If psychoanalytic theory is to be believed, they are already imprinted with an invisible network of drives which bind their bodies to those of others, and which will prove a constant source of affliction to them.

Original sin is not the legacy of our first parents but of our parents, who in turn inherited it from their own. The past is what we are made of. Throngs of ghostly ancestors lurk within our most casual gestures, preprogramming our desires and flicking our actions mischievously awry. Because our earliest, most passionate love affair takes place when we are helpless infants, it is caught up with frustration and voracious need. And this means that our loving will always be defective. As with the doctrine of original sin, this condition lies at the core of the self, yet is nobody's responsibility. Love is both what we need in order to flourish and what we are born to fail at. Our only hope is learning to fail better. Which may, of course, prove not to be good enough.

Jean-Jacques Rousseau, then, was mistaken to believe that human beings are born free. But this does not mean that they are born sinful either. No creature without language, which is what "infant" means, could be that. As the theologian Herbert McCabe writes, "Everybody is immaculately conceived."[4] Even so, it is true that the moral dice are scarcely loaded in our favour. Infants are innocent (literally, harmless) in the way that tortoises are, not in the way that adults who refuse to turn a machine gun on civilians are. Their innocence does them no particular credit. We are born self-centred as an effect of our biology. Egoism is a natural condition, whereas goodness involves a set of complex practical skills we have to learn. Men and women are thrust at birth into a deep mutual dependence—a truth scandalous to Rousseau, who in his petit-bourgeois way placed an excessive value on human autonomy. But original sin means that any such total autonomy is a myth. As such, it is a radical sort of notion. It questions the individualist doctrine that we are the sole proprietors of our own actions. Among other things, it is an argument against capital punishment. This is not to deny responsibility, simply to insist that our actions are no more inalienable than our property. Who can say for sure, in the great skein of human action and reaction, who really has ownership of a particular deed? Who exactly is responsible for killing the saintly Simon in *Lord of the Flies*? It is not always easy to say where my responsibility (or even interests, desires, or identity) ends and yours begins. Can't "who is acting here?" or even "who is desiring here?" be an intelligible question?

There is, to be sure, more than this to the idea of original sin. We must also keep in mind, as I have written elsewhere, "the perversity of human desire, the prevalence of illusion and idolatry, the scandal of suffering, the dull persistence of oppression and injustice, the scarcity of public virtue, the insolence of power, the fragility of goodness and the formidable power of appetite and self-interest."[5] None of this means that we are powerless to transform our current condition. It means, rather, that we shall not do so without soberly acknowledging our dispiriting history. This is not a history which rules out the possibility of, say, socialism or feminism. But it does rule out the possibility of utopia. There are certain negative features of the human species which cannot be greatly altered. As long as there is love and death, for example, the tragedy of mourning those dear to us who perish will know no end. It is almost certain that we cannot root out violence without also sabotaging certain capacities we value. But though death and suffering may be beyond our powers to annul, the same is not true of social injustice.

Besides, that certain things cannot be changed is far from a bad thing. Only a social order which makes a fetish of the new is likely to deny this. To think in this way is one of the many misconceptions of postmodernism. We cannot alter the fact that infants need nourishing, but this is no reason to gnash our teeth. Not all permanence is an offence against the political left. Continuity is at least as significant a factor in history as change, and many continuities are to be cherished. It would appear to be a persistent feature of human cultures that great masses of people are not regularly slaughtered simply because the moon is full, but not even postmodernists should feel down in the mouth about this. Durability is no more precious or worthless in itself than is change. The assumption that change is radical whereas the unchanging is conservative is an illusion. Richard J. Bernstein writes that we must resist the temptation to see evil as "a fixed ontological feature of the human condition,"[6] since this means confessing that there is nothing to be done about it. We just have to live with it. Yet it does not follow that because something is a persistent feature of the human condition, there is nothing to be done about it. Illness is one such enduring feature, but this does not persuade doctors to give up curing the sick in a fit of fatalism. People will probably always engage in bloodthirsty conflict, but this does not mean that we should not strive to resolve such contentions. A desire for justice might well be a constant feature of the human condition. Certainly the historical record would suggest so. Fixed ontological features are not always to be lamented. It is dogmatic, and thus not in the spirit of mutability, to believe so.

An equally purblind postmodern dogma holds that difference and diversity are always to be commended. No doubt this is often the case. But the blunt truth is that if the human race had been made up almost entirely of gay Latinos, with just a few heterosexual deviants thrown in here and there to keep the species ticking over, a great deal of mayhem and massacre would almost certainly have been avoided. No doubt gay Latinos would long since have split into a thousand rival sects, each armed to the teeth and distinguished from its fellows by the slimmest nuances of lifestyle. But this partisanship would be nothing to what tends to happen when one group of humans encounters another group with blatantly different markings. Of course these dissensions are largely political in form. But it is unlikely they will be resolved unless we acknowledge our built-in tendency to experience fear, insecurity, and antagonism in the presence of potential predators, a tendency which no doubt has eminently useful evolutionary functions.

Let us return, however, to the idea of original sin. Sammy Mountjoy, the hero of Golding's *Free Fall*, sets out to unravel the unfathomably intricate text of his own existence, seeking to pinpoint the moment when he lost his freedom. (Mountjoy is the name of a prison in Dublin.) He is out to trace what he calls "the awful line of descent" by which guilt is transmitted like a highly contagious virus from one human being to another. "We are neither the innocent nor the wicked," Sammy reflects. "We are the guilty. We fall down. We crawl on hands and knees. We weep and tear each other." But the Fall was never just a moment, and it is never simply in the past. Sammy has destroyed his lover Beatrice, and he is now taking soundings in "this ocean of cause and effect which is Beatrice and me." But he, too, was torn apart as a child by a frustrated schoolmistress, who was in love with the pedophilic priest who adopted him. And so the entangled web of injury and guilt, action and reaction, ramifies endlessly. This state of negative solidarity, as one might call it, shades off indefinitely in every direction.

For Golding's novel, only an act of forgiveness can break this toxic line of descent, cutting the knot and prising open the deadly circuit of cause and effect. So Sammy returns to his childhood home to forgive his schoolteacher, only to find that she has suppressed her sadistic treatment of him and escaped into innocence. The innocent cannot forgive, the narrator observes, because they do not know that they have been offended. Mountjoy is consequently left with his guilt on his back. In the end, his sadistic teacher has the upper hand. Beatrice, likewise, had lapsed into madness and is beyond moral reach. What will really break the lethal line of descent is not Sammy's forgiving but his being forgiven. It is when he is shown mercy in a Nazi prisoner-of-war camp, released from a broom cupboard where he is crazed with terror, that the novel is able to conclude.

If *Pincher Martin* is a fable of purgatory, Flann O'Brien's *The Third Policeman* is an allegory of hell. In this most gloriously fantastic and perverse of Irish fictions, it is not the protagonist who dies in the first few pages, but the narrator himself. He has set out with an accomplice to rob old farmer Mathers of the cash box which he keeps concealed under the floorboards of his living room; but when he thrusts his arm under the floorboards to grope for the box, he is overtaken by a most curious sensation:

> I cannot hope to describe what it was but it had frightened me very much long before I had under-stood it even slightly. It was some change which came upon me or upon the room, indescribably subtle, yet momentous, ineffable. It was as if the daylight had changed with unnatural suddenness, as if the temperature of the evening had altered greatly in an instant or as if the air had become twice as rare or twice as dense as it had been in the winking of an eye; perhaps all of these and other things happened together for all my senses were bewildered all at once and could give me no expla-

nation. The fingers of my right hand, thrust into the opening in the floor, had closed mechanically, found nothing at all and come up again empty. The box was gone!

Hearing a soft cough behind him, the narrator turns to find the farmer whose head he has just smashed in with a spade eyeing him silently from his chair in the corner. The reader discovers later that the narrator's accomplice has already removed the cash box, and in order to keep its contents for himself has replaced it with a bomb. The bomb has exploded, and the narrator is right to feel that some momentous transformation has come over him because he has just been blown to pieces.

In groping for the cash box, O'Brien's narrator finds "nothing at all"; and during his ensuing conversation with the dead-but-alive farmer, he gradually realises that every reply the old man gives to his questions is couched in the negative. "There is a lot to be said for No as a general principle," Mathers observes, perhaps echoing the Irish novelist Laurence Sterne's comment in *Tristram Shandy* that one should show some respect for nothingness, considering what worse things there are in the world. In a similar vein, the greatest of Irish philosophers, Bishop Berkeley, declared that something and nothing were closely allied. "I have decided," Mathers informs the narrator, "to say No henceforth to every suggestion, request or inquiry whether inward or outward . . . I have refused more requests and negatived more statements than any man living or dead. I have rejected, reneged, disagreed, refused and denied to an extent that is unbelievable."

The world of *The Third Policeman* is one of surreal impossibilities. Bicycles and their riders, for example, come by a subtle process of osmosis to intermingle their atoms and stealthily assume one another's characteristics. Men are to be found leaning casually up against fireplaces as though resting on their handlebars. One offending bicycle has to be hanged, an operation which involves building a bicycle-shaped coffin. The novel is stuffed with metaphysical paradoxes and conundrums, several of them revolving on ideas of nothingness, void, and infinity. Once he is dead, the narrator himself becomes nameless (though we never knew his name in the first place). For some cryptic reason, lacking a name disqualifies him from owning a watch. There are mock-erudite allusions to a certain French scholar, de Selby, who believes that the darkness of night consists in some tangible black substance, a dusky stuff which he attempts to bottle. Sleep he sees as a succession of fainting fits brought on by semiasphyxiation due to this noxious "staining of the atmosphere." In de Selby's thought, nothing becomes something. It is as though he cannot bear the idea of pure absence.

There are further Escher-like images of warping and nullity—a room in a police station which has no size at all, another police station tucked inside the wall of a house, a group of objects without dimensions and of indefinable colour. Policeman McCruiskeen fashions a series of small boxes, some so tiny as to be invisible. The tools with which he manufactures them are also too miniscule to be perceptible. "The one I am making now," he informs the narrator, "is nearly as small as nothing. [Box] Number One would hold a million of them at the same time and there would be room left for a pair of woman's horse-breeches if they were rolled up. The dear knows where it will stop and terminate." To which the narrator replies, courteously if a touch prosaically, "Such work must be very hard on the eyes."

McCruiskeen also manages to prick the narrator's hand with a spear which does not apparently touch it. This is because the point of the spear is not the actual point, simply the bit of the point which is visible to the human eye. "What you think is the point," McCruiskeen explains, "is not the point at all but only the beginning of the sharpness . . . The point is seven inches long and it is so sharp and thin that you cannot see it with the old eye. The first half of the sharpness is thick and strong but you cannot see it either because the real sharpness runs into it and if you saw the one you could see the other or maybe you could notice the joint." The real point, he remarks, is "so thin that it could go into your hand and out in the other extremity externally and you would not feel a bit of it and you would see nothing and hear nothing. It is so thin that maybe it does not exist at all and you could spend half an hour trying to think about it and you could put no thought around it in the end." Simply trying to conceive how sharp the real point is, the metaphysically minded policeman advises, will cause you "to hurt your box [brain] with the excruciation of it." The scene confirms the argument of the Irish philosopher Edmund Burke that the sublime—that which defeats thought or representation—can be very small as well as immensely large. Mc-Cruiskeen's diminutive spears and boxes slip through the net of language, just as the Almighty is said to do.

One would expect an intensely religious culture like that of O'Brien's Ireland to take a certain interest in the void. After all, God is pictured by the greatest of all medieval Irish thinkers, John Scottus Eriugena, as pure vacuity. Eriugena, who was probably not the world's most charismatic teacher (he is said to have been stabbed to death by his students with their pens), is as keen on negating and rebutting as old Mathers himself.[7] God in his view can be defined only in terms of what he is not. Even to call him good or wise or all-powerful is to translate him into our own terms, and thus to falsify him. Eriugena, like Thomas Aquinas, would have heartily agreed with the atheists who claim that when people discuss God they have no idea what they are talking about. He was influenced in this view by the ancient philosopher Pseudo-Dionysus, whose discourse on God in *The Divine Names* is one of resolute denial: "He was not. He will not be. He did not come to be. He is not in the midst of becoming. He will not come to be. No. He is not."[8] Only the finite can be defined; and since human subjectivity for Eriugena is infinite, as a sharing in the unfathomable abyss of the godhead, it follows that the human, too, eludes all definition.

If God is non-being, then so in essence are his creatures. To belong to him is to share in his nullity. There is a nothingness at the heart of the self which makes it what it is. Human beings for Eriugena are necessarily inscrutable to themselves. They can never get a total grip on their own natures, because there is nothing stable or determinate enough about them to be securely known. As such, they are as elusive as the Freudian unconscious. We have complete self-knowledge, Eriugena comments, only when we do not know who we are.

God's perfect freedom lies at the root of human freedom. Just as God is boundless, so in Eriugena's opinion are we. We partake of his infinite liberty by belonging to him. Paradoxically, it is by being dependent on the Creator that we become free and autonomous—rather as it is by trusting in a reliable parent that we can eventually enter upon our own selfhood. Eriugena is a kind of spiritual anarchist. Like God, human beings are in his view a law unto themselves. They are their own ground, cause, end, and origin, just as their Maker is. And they are like this because they are his creation, made in his own image and likeness.

In an audacious move, Eriugena assigns the human mind a notably higher status than was customary in medieval thought. The human animal has a godlike power to create and annihilate. For this medieval philosopher, as for the poet

William Blake, to see material things with visionary clarity is to grasp that their roots run down to infinity. Eternity, as Blake remarks, is in love with the products of time. For evil, by contrast, finite things are an obstacle to the infinity of will or desire, and so must be annihilated. Creation for the evil-minded is a stain or blemish on the purity of the infinite. The German philosopher Schelling saw evil as far more spiritual than he saw good. For him, it represented a bleak, barren hatred of material reality. We shall see later that this was more or less how the Nazis felt as well.

The world, Eriugena considered, was a kind of exuberant dance, without end or purpose. It would not be a bad description of the novels of his later compatriot James Joyce. The cosmos has something of the whorling, spiraling, self-involved quality of traditional Celtic art. Like such art, it exists purely for its own self-delight, not to accomplish some mighty goal. And this is the surest sign that it springs from God, who is equally without point or purpose. Like Joyce's fiction, the world is not designed to get anywhere in particular. For Eriugena, as for some modern physics, Nature is a dynamic process which varies according to the observer's shifting vantage point. It is an infinity of partial perspectives, an endless sport of multiple viewpoints. There are traces of this vision in the thought of the Dublin philosopher Bishop Berkeley five centuries later. There is little that modern philosophers like Friedrich Nietzsche or Jacques Derrida could have taught this audacious medieval Irishman. For holding these views, Eriugena had the honour of being condemned for heresy. The infinite freedom of the individual was not quite what the thirteenth century papacy wanted to hear.

It comes as no surprise, then, that *The Third Policeman* is much taken with whirling atoms and spiraling circles. The Sergeant observes that "everything is composed of small particles of itself and they are flying around in concentric circles and arcs and segments and innumerable other geometrical figures too numerous to mention collectively, never standing still or resting but spinning away and darting hither and thither and back again, all the time on the go. These diminutive gentlemen are called atoms." It is not far from Eriugena's vision of the cosmos. The world is made up mostly of nothing. In that sense, it is hard to say whether it is more like heaven or hell. Things dart hither and thither and back again without ever getting anywhere, as does *The Third Policeman* itself. At the end of the story, the narrator finds himself back at the police station he left earlier, a place described in exactly the same words which were used when he first encountered it. This eerie passage evokes the ending of *Pincher Martin,* as the rock, sky, and ocean of Martin's super-solid world are shown to be so much painted paper:

> There was a bend in the road and when I came round it an extraordinary spectacle was presented to me. About a hundred yards away was a house

which astonished me. It looked as if it were painted like an advertisement on a board on the roadside and, indeed, very poorly painted. It looked completely false and unconvincing. It did not seem to have any depth or breadth and looked as if it would not deceive a child. That was not in itself sufficient to surprise me because I had seen pictures and notices by the roadside before. What bewildered me was the sure knowledge, deeply rooted in my mind, that this was the house I was searching for and that there were people inside it. I had never seen with my eyes ever in my life before anything so unnatural and appalling and my gaze faltered about the thing uncomprehendingly as if one of the customary dimensions were missing, leaving no meaning in the remainder. The appearance of the house was the greatest surprise I had encountered ever, and I felt afraid of it.

Some of the main features of evil are assembled here: its uncanniness, its appalling unreality, its surprisingly superficial nature, its assault on meaning, the fact that it lacks some vital dimension, the way it is trapped in the mind-numbing monotony of an eternal recurrence. O'Brien's narrator is in hell, and must forever trudge back to the beginning of the book once he has stumbled to the end. The damned are those who are dead but won't lie down. To this extent, they bear an uncanny resemblance to the Jesus who is supposed to have redeemed the world.

Eriugena sees time as looped upon itself rather than as an endless series. So does James Joyce in *Finnegans Wake,* or W. B. Yeats in his mythologies. The most celebrated of all Irish dramas, *Waiting for Godot,* was once described as a play in which "nothing happens—twice." A sense of time as cyclical is common in Irish culture. But what these writers regard as a kind of cosmic exuberance, as the world curves back sportively on itself rather than plodding doggedly onward, turns out in *The Third Policeman* to be the most terrible fate of all. To see time as spiraling upon itself belongs in one sense to a vision of virtue. It resists the mechanistic view for which every act exists only for the sake of some other act. This is the twilight existence of those angst-ridden men and women who, in D. H. Lawrence's phrase, are "unable to live on the spot where they are"—bankers, corporate executives, politicians, and other such mortally endangered souls. But cyclical time also belongs to a vision of evil—to a world in which the damned are those who have lost the capacity to die and, being unable to make an end, are doomed to eternal repetition. Slavoj Žižek points out that immortality is usually associated with goodness, but that the truth is actually the reverse. The primordial immortality is that of evil: "Evil is something which threatens to return for ever," Žižek writes, "a spectral dimension which magically survives its physical annihilation and continues to haunt us."[9] There is a kind of "obscene infinity" about evil—a refusal to accept our mortality as natural, material beings. Lots of men and women hope to live forever; the damned are those for whom this seductive dream has become atrociously real.

In a bold mixture of literary modes, Graham Greene's novel *Brighton Rock* sets a figure of absolute evil in the context of cheap boardinghouse Brighton. The novel is a blend of gangland thriller and metaphysical meditation, a risky enterprise of uneven success. It is not easy to portray a character who seems to live both in hell and the Home Counties.

Is the small-time gangster Pinkie to be seen as demonic in his hostility to human life, or is he just another alienated adolescent? The novel's own answer is unequivocal: as far as Greene is concerned, this seventeen-year-old hoodlum is damned from the outset. If he lives physically in a louche world of tarts, mobsters, and cheap seaside entertainment, his spiritual abode is in eternity; and the two worlds can never intersect. We are told by Greene in a lurid rhetorical gesture that Pinkie's "slatey eyes were touched with the annihilating eternity from which he had come and to which he went." The evil are not really there. They have a problem in being present. Hannah Arendt notes the "remoteness from reality" of Hitler's henchman Adolf Eichmann.[10] When Pinkie dies, "it was as if he'd been withdrawn suddenly by a hand out of any existence—past or present, whipped away into zero—nothing."

He falls to his death from a cliff into the sea, but nobody hears the sound of the impact. There is nothing of enough substance to make one. His death does not make much of a splash.

Just as Pincher Martin is literally dead, Pinkie is spiritually so. He is a fine example of Nietzsche's nihilist, who has "a will to nothingness, an aversion to life," and acts out "a rebellion against the most fundamental presuppositions of life."[11] Like Pincher Martin, he betrays an incapacity for any kind of life beyond exploiting others for his own destructive ends. Unlike one's average teenager gangster, he is as remote from everyday sensual existence as a Carthusian monk. He does not dance, smoke, drink, gamble, joke, eat chocolate, or have friends. He detests Nature, and has a squeamish horror of sex. "To marry," he thinks to himself, "it was like ordure on the hands." His mode of life is as immaterial as infinity. He is not only aloof and austere, but virulently hostile to the material world as such. And this, as we shall see, is characteristic of evil. It is as though some vital piece of the youth has been cut out. He lacks all sympathetic imagination, unable to conceive what others are feeling. He is as unschooled in the language of the emotions as he is in Hindi. Other people's behaviour seems to him as indecipherable as a flea's might appear to us. There is more than a touch of the psychopath about him.

The fact that this minor hoodlum is only seventeen might account for his lack of experience. But the spiritual vacuity inside him runs much deeper than youthful ignorance. As such, it goes to confirm a certain ideological thesis underlying the novel: the belief that evil is a timeless condition rather than a matter of social circumstance. Pinkie was presumably as blank at the age of four as he is now. You can have this kind of evil at any age, just as you can have chicken pox at any age. Pinkie is not evil because he kills people; he kills people because he is evil. He was presumably born malignant; but this does not modify his nastiness in the eyes of his author, as we have suggested already that it should.

There is much play in the novel on ideas of ignorance, innocence, and experience, and Pinkie falls squarely into the first category. There is a "horrifying ignorance" or "soured virginity" about him, which causes him to observe human affairs with the blank incomprehension of a Venusian. He has the worthless purity of those who have never lived. As one critic has put it, it is his "inability to belong to his own experience" which is so striking. Human intimacy looms up for him as a hideous invasion of his being, rather as the penetrating black lightning does for Pincher Martin. Both characters experience love as a horrifying demand to which they know they are utterly unequal. Passions are predatory: when Pinkie feels some faint stirrings of sexual pleasure with his girlfriend Rose, "an enormous pressure beat on him; it was like something trying to get in; the pressure of gigantic wings against the glass." "He was like a child with haemophilia," comments the narrator: "every contact drew blood."

It is important to the novel that Pinkie is a religious

believer, as Pincher Martin is not. Greene makes it plain that his hero believes in hell and damnation, and (just possibly) in heaven as well, though he is rather more sceptical on this score. In a similar way, Thomas Mann's damned Adrian Leverkühn, whom we shall be considering in a moment, chooses as a young man to study theology. To be damned, you must know what it is you are turning down, rather as you must be of sound mind to get married. Even Pincher Martin comes in the end to realise what is afoot, as his cry of defiance to God makes clear. If Golding does not make Martin say something like "I shit on your heaven!" he cannot be consigned to hell. It would be unforgivably absentminded of the Almighty to pack off some of his creatures to everlasting torment without having alerted them to this disagreeable possibility in the first place. You cannot end up in hell by accident, any more than you can learn Portuguese by accident.

The theological point at stake here is that God does not damn anyone to hell. You land yourself there by turning down his love, if such a rebuff is conceivable. It is the final, terrifying consequence of human freedom. God cannot be responsible for being stood up. As Pinkie puts it, "God couldn't escape the evil mouth which chose to eat its own damnation." In this sense, the Creator is at the mercy of his creatures. Consigning yourself to perdition is your final malicious triumph over the Almighty. It is, to be sure, a Pyrrhic sort of victory, like chopping off your head to escape being guillotined. But there is no other way of outsmarting God. It is the only effective way of having him over a barrel.

To put one over on God is to get on terms with him; and in *Brighton Rock,* this is one of several ways in which good and evil display a secret affinity. Another shared characteristic is that both can involve a lack of know-how. We have seen this already in Pinkie's case; but it is also true of Rose, whose goodness thrives on her virginal lack of acquaintance with the world. It is significant that no figure in the novel is both virtuous and experienced. Good and evil alike transcend everyday existence. Both Pinkie and Rose have the dogmatic absolutism of the ingénue, and each signifies a different kind of nullity. Pinkie represents the void or antilife of evil, while Rose is a kind of vacuum because her goodness thrives on her greenness. To this extent, the two are allies as well as antagonists. "Good and evil lived in the same country," remarks the narrator, "spoke the same language, came together like old friends." If it is true that God has a special love for the sinner, then it follows that the damned must be especially dear to him. In this sense, evil is a deviant image of divine love, as plain immorality is not. If there is no saintliness around to remind you of God, there is at least a negative image of him available, known as sheer unadulterated wickedness.

There is thus a touch of privilege about evil. Pinkie despises the world in the style of a spiritual aristocrat. He is a kind of nihilist, and the nihilist is the supreme artist. He is an artist because he conjures into being a nothingness so pure that it beggars all other works of creation, with their material blemishes and imperfections. To sin in a big way is to rise above mere common or garden virtue. Lapsed or heterodox Catholics like Greene himself may be sinners, but at least they are more spiritually glamorous than the boringly well-behaved. Being thrown out of an exclusive club beats not being invited to join in the first place. The evil must know about transcendence in order to turn it down, whereas the merely ethical would not recognise it if it fell into their laps.

There is another way in which there is a secret compact between Pinkie and Rose, the priestly criminal and the credulous virgin. Because she is purely good, Rose forgives Pinkie even though she is aware that he is a murderer. The good accept evil by embracing it in their love and mercy. In taking it upon themselves, however, they are drawn inexorably into its orbit. The tragic scapegoat is a case in point. Christ, for example, may not have been sinful, but Saint Paul observes that he was "made sin" for the sake of humanity. A redeemer must know in his bones what he is redeeming, rather than being monkishly remote from it. Otherwise the situation cannot be salvaged from the inside, which is the only form of salvation that works.

Being on speaking terms with evil is where the saints have the edge over what one might call the moral middle classes. The latter group are represented in *Brighton Rock* by Ida Arnold, a meddling moralist who preens herself smugly on knowing the difference between right and wrong. Blowsy, carnal, big-hearted and worldly wise, Ida stands for the suburban morality for which the metaphysical Pinkie and Rose have nothing but contempt. "She's just nothing," Pinkie snarls, adding later, "She couldn't burn if she tried." Right and wrong can't hold a candle to good and evil. Ida is too vulgar for hellfire. She is full of shop-soiled wisdom and tarnished moral clichés. The secular ethics she represents are strong on the duties of a citizen, but baffled in the face of salvation and damnation. Ida is a day-tripper from the land of pragmatic morality who has blundered into absolutist terrain. And the novel itself, even though it writes Pinkie off as unregenerate, thoroughly shares his contempt for her. The Ida Arnolds of this world, like T. S. Eliot's Hollow Men, are too shallow even to be damned. When it comes to respectable morality, it is hard not to feel that Greene himself is squarely on the side of evil, for the most spiritually elitist of reasons. It is not for nothing that he remained a loyal friend of the "treasonable" double agent Kim Philby, in the teeth of Establishment disapproval.

Brighton Rock thus helps to reinforce one particularly dubious myth about evil—that there is a kind of down-at-heel heroism about it, as with the Satan of Milton's *Paradise Lost*. Better to reign in hell than spend your time nattering indignantly about right and wrong in squalid Brighton cafes. The novel morally rejects its own hero. But at the same time it harbours a view of evil which reflects his own way of seeing. Pinkie is written off by the novel for his inability to surrender himself to human life; but human life in the novel is nowhere shown as being worth surrendering to. He cannot understand everyday human reality, but the tawdry common existence presented by the narrative is not worth understanding in any case. The only image of authentic love we are given—Rose—is just as indifferent to the commonplace as her demoniac boyfriend. We are left with a compelling image of a man eternally estranged from creaturely existence. For a much finer portrayal, we can turn to Thomas Mann's *Doctor Faustus,* a novel in which we hear the music of the damned.

Adrian Leverkühn, the doomed composer of Mann's work, represents a dramatic twist to the idea of evil as self-destruction. He deliberately infects himself with syphilis by visiting a prostitute, and does so in order to conjure resplendent musical visions from the gradual degeneration of his brain. In this way, Leverkühn seeks to turn his hellish disease into the transcendent glory of his art. "What madness, what deliberate, reckless tempting of God," reflects Mann's horrified narrator, "what compulsion to comprise the punishment in the sin, finally what deep, deeply mysterious longing for daemonic Dionysian conception, for a deathly unchaining of chemical change in his nature was at work, that having been warned he despised the warning and insisted upon possession of this flesh [of a syphilitic prostitute]?"

Adrian is a Dionysian artist, plumbing the depths of human wretchedness in order to pluck order from chaos. His art strives to wrest the spirit from the flesh, wholeness from affliction, the angelic from the demonic. If the artist seeks to redeem a corrupt world by the transfigurative power of his art, then he or she must be on intimate terms with evil. This is why the modern artist is the secular version of Christ, who descends into the hell of despair and destitution in order to gather it into eternal life. As W. B. Yeats writes, it is "in the foul rag and bone shop of the heart" that art has its unlovely root. Like Yeats, Mann's hero believes that "nothing can be sole or whole / That has not been rent." As a character in Dostoevsky's *The Brothers Karamazov* remarks of the dissolute Dmitri Karamazov: "The experience of ultimate degradation is as vital to such unruly, dissolute natures as the experience of sheer goodness." The artist must be on nodding terms with evil because he must treat all experience as grist to the mill of his art, whatever its conventional moral value. This is why, if his work is to flourish, he himself must be a kind of immoralist, reluctantly abandoning all hope of sainthood. It is as though his art sucks all the goodness out of him. The more magnificent the art, the more degenerate the life. The late nineteenth century is full of parallels between the artist— doped, debauched, anguished, absinthe-sodden—and the Satanist. Both figures are equally scandalous to the reputable middle classes. And one reason for this is that both art and evil exist for their own sake. Neither will have any truck with utility or exchange value.

Leverkühn, then, presses death and disease into the service of artistic life. In Freud's rather more technical terms, he harnesses *Thanatos,* or the death drive, to the cause of *Eros,* or the life instincts. But the price he pays for this pact with the devil is an exorbitant one. The life he creates—his magnificent music—is cerebral, emotionally disabled, shot through with mockery, nihilism, and Satanic pride. Its frigid self-parodies are bereft of all human sympathy. There is something inhuman about this music's very virtuosity, marked as it is by a vein of "diabolical cleverness." As the ultimate aesthete, Leverkühn literally sacrifices his existence for art. But those who spurn life for art will leave a chilling trace of that sacrifice in their art; so that there is something self-defeating as well as perversely heroic about this project.

Leverkühn's fate is an allegory of Nazi Germany, a nation which also infected itself with poison, and which grew drunk on fantasies of omnipotence before plunging to its ruin. It was, remarks the narrator, "a profligate dictatorship vowed to nihilism from its beginnings." With fascism, writes Walter Benjamin, "self-alienation has reached such a degree that [humanity] can experience its own destruction as an aesthetic pleasure of the first order."[12] It is from his own self-destruction that Leverkühn reaps the aesthetic triumph of his music.

Evil, as we shall see, is bound up with destruction in several senses. One bond between them is that fact that destruction is really the only way to trump God's act of creation. Evil would actually prefer that there was nothing at all, since it does not see the point of created things. It loathes them because, as Thomas Aquinas claims, being is itself a kind of good. The more richly abundant existence is, the more value there is in the world. The simple fact that there are turnips, telecommunications, and feelings of excited anticipation around the place is a good thing. (What about bird flu and genocide, though? We shall come to this problem later on.)

Evil, however, does not see things this way. "All that comes to birth / Is fit for overthrow, as nothing worth," observes Mephistopheles in Goethe's *Faust*. The prospect of nuclear holocaust, or of the world being swamped by its own oceans, turns evil weak at the knees with delight. When a friend of Pinkie in *Brighton Rock* remarks in his bar-stool-wise way that "the world's got to go on," Pinkie's bemused response is "Why?" It is sometimes said that the most fundamental question we can raise is, "Why is there anything at all, rather than nothing?" Pinkie's own reply to this question would be a sardonic "Why indeed?" What's the point of it all? Isn't the material world incurably banal and monotonous, and wouldn't it be far better off not existing? The philosopher Arthur Schopenhauer certainly thought so. Nothing struck him as more self-evidently foolish than the assumption that the human race was a good idea.

Given the intolerable fact that things do exist, however, the best evil can do is try to annihilate them. In this way, it can seek to get on terms with God by inverting his act of creation, in a grisly parody of the Book of Genesis. Creation out of nothing can only be the work of an absolute power. But there is something just as absolute about the act of destruction. Just as an act of creation can never be repeated, neither can an act of destruction. You cannot smash the same priceless Chinese vase twice, as opposed to smashing a reconstruction of it. Demolishing can be as enthralling as creating, as toddlers are well aware. Heaving a brick through a stained-glass window can be quite as agreeable as designing the thing in the first place.

Even so, evil can never quite get even with the Almighty, which is one reason why Satan is in such a permanent sulk. For it depends on there being material things in the first place in order to be able to put its foot through them. To invert the act of creation cannot help paying it a certain grudging homage. As Sebastian Barry writes in his novel *The Secret Scripture:* "The devil's own tragedy is he is the author of nothing and architect of empty spaces." If it is true, as a character in *Doctor Faustus* remarks, that "everything happens in God, most of all the falling from him," then the Almighty preempts those who rebel against him at every turn. He is like a club you cannot resign from. To revolt against him is inevitably to acknowledge his existence. And this, for evil, is a source of infinite frustration. The slogan of Milton's Satan—"Evil, be thou my good!"—suggests that good takes precedence over evil at the very moment that evil tries to oust it.

In a similar way, Adrian Leverkühn's music is a product

of genius, but much of it is more parodic than original. It feeds off already created forms, mocking and travestying them just as evil does. Like all avant-garde activity, it cannot help perpetuating the past in the very act of trying to blow it to bits. In this respect, evil is always belated with regard to good. It is parasitic on the very world it abhors. Goetz, the hero of Jean-Paul Sartre's play *Lucifer and the Lord,* praises evil because it is the only thing God has left to humanity to create, having cornered all the more positive stuff himself. Evil believes that it is entirely self-dependent, conjuring itself up out of nothing, but the truth is that it is not its own origin. Something has always come before it. And this is one reason why it is eternally miserable. Satan himself is a fallen angel, a being created by God, even if he is what his psychotherapist might call in denial about it.

In destroying himself, Leverkühn steps into God's shoes. This is because the suicide exercises a quasi-divine power over his own existence. Not even God can prevent him from doing away with himself, which is where he is most gloriously, pointlessly free. Freedom can be used to negate itself, as it was by the Nazis. The highest freedom in this view is to abnegate freedom. If you can surrender the most precious possession you have, you must be mighty indeed. God is vulnerable to the free activities of his own creatures. He is powerless to prevent them from spitting in his face. Self-destruction is the phony victory of those who cannot forgive him for giving them life. You can always get your own back on God by laying violent hands on yourself. If there is nothing much inside you in the first place, this may turn out to be no great loss.

Like Pinkie, Leverkühn knows all about theology. In fact, he chooses to study it at university. But he does so, he confesses, sheerly out of arrogance. Besides, it is always wise to bone up on the competition. Like Pinkie, too, he is monkish, cerebral, and aloof, prone to disgust with life and revolted by physical contact. Hitler was said to feel much the same way about physical touching. Leverkühn, we are told, "shrank from every connection with the actual because he saw therein a theft from the possible." The actual—the fleshly and finite—he can see only as an obstacle to the infinite will. It stands in the way of his Faustian craving for a godlike knowledge and artistry. Finite things are a scandal to his disembodied dreams of infinity. All actual achievement is automatically trivial. In this Manichean view, the Creation and the Fall are one, in the sense that anything that exists must thereby be corrupt. "Nothing has killed itself, creation is its wound," remarks Danton in Georg Büchner's great drama *Danton's Death*. Matter is simply what is left behind by the death of nothingness. It is as though it is standing in for what should ideally be a gap.

To the Faustian mind, any particular achievement is bound to appear like nothing, in contrast to the infinity of everything. The boundlessness of your desire reduces the actual objects of your longing to mere bagatelles. Evil is therefore sure to reject God, since God, according to Saint Augustine, is where the infinity of human desire eventually comes to rest. And such rest is intolerable to the ravenous will, which must remain eternally sullen and dissatisfied. Goethe's Faust will be consigned to the clutches of Mephistopheles the moment he ceases to strive. So the infinity of the will comes to replace the eternity of God. And this is scarcely a profitable exchange. For eternity, to quote William Blake, is in love with the products of time, whereas this manic will is secretly in love only with itself. It despises the world in its glacially superior way, and yearns only to perpetuate itself for all eternity. It is thus, as we shall see later, very close to what Freud calls the death drive.

Evil, then, is a form of transcendence, even if from the point of view of good it is a transcendence gone awry. Perhaps it is the only form of transcendence left in a postreligious world. We know nothing any more of choirs of heavenly hosts, but we know about Auschwitz. Maybe all that now survives of God is this negative trace of him known as wickedness, rather as all that may survive of some great symphony is the silence which it imprints on the air like an inaudible sound as it shimmers to a close. Perhaps evil is all that now keeps warm the space where God used to be. As Mann's narrator observes of one of Adrian's musical compositions: "A work that deals with the Tempter, with apostasy, with damnation, what else could it be but a religious work?" If evil really is the last surviving remnant of God, it is bound to appeal to those like Leverkühn who want to kick free of the world but no longer believe in a heaven. Like good, evil makes a statement not just about this or that piece of reality, but about reality as such. Both conditions are in this sense metaphysical. Where they differ is in their judgments on the inherent goodness or otherwise of existence.

There is, then, what the narrator calls a kind of "aristocratic nihilism" about Mann's protagonist. He is cool, ironic, and bafflingly self-contained. The novel speaks of his "luciferian sardonic mood." There is nothing sensuous in his nature. He takes no delight in the visual, and if he chooses music as his field it is because it is the most purely formal of the arts. Modernist or experimental art, of the kind Leverkühn creates, represents the point at which art ceases to draw its content from the world around it. Instead, it begins to turn in on itself and investigate its own forms, taking itself as its subject matter. Leverkühn is a formalist because he is fearful of content, which in its obtrusive way would simply baulk his drive for the infinite. Søren Kierkegaard speaks in *The Concept of Anxiety* of "the dreadful emptiness and contentlessness of evil."[13] The purest form, one most free of all content, is a void. But since chaos is a kind of void as well, pure form and pure disorder are hard to tell apart. Some modernist poets professed to believe that the most accomplished poem was a blank page. Nothing is less vulnerable or obstructive than nothing. This is why those who are allergic to material reality are so deeply in love with vacancy. The final triumph of the free spirit would be the annihilation of the whole world. Then the world cannot intervene between you and your desire. It is in this sense that desire, in the end, is for nothing at all.

For theology, as we have seen in the case of Eriugena, God is also pure nothingness. He is not a material entity or an extraterrestrial object. He cannot be located either inside or outside the universe. Indeed, he, too, is a formalist in his own exotic fashion. The language he speaks, one resonant through his Creation, is known as mathematics. It is the key to the laws of the universe, but it is entirely without content. It is purely a matter of the manipulation of signs. Mathematics is all form and no substance. In this sense it has a close affinity with music. But God's negativity is not such that it cannot stomach the fleshly and finite. Instead, as Blake suggests, he is besotted with material things. The Christian belief is that God achieves supreme self-expression in a tortured human body. He is present in the form of flesh, but above all in the form of mangled flesh.

Hell sounds alarmingly real, but as we have seen in the case of Pincher Martin, it is really a kind of vacuity. It signifies a raging, vindictive fury at existence as such. "This is the secret delight and security of hell," we read in *Doctor Faustus*, "that it is not to be informed on, that it is protected from speech, that it just is, but cannot be made public in the newspaper . . . for there everything ends—not only the words that describe but everything altogether." Hell is as far beyond the reach of language as the symbolist poet's blank page. It has the enigmatic quality of things that are brutely, unambiguously themselves. Things that are purely themselves slip through the net of language and cannot be spoken of. As Ludwig Wittgenstein remarks in his *Philosophical Investigations,* there is no more useless proposition than the identity of a thing with itself. The same is true of the kind of modernist or experimental works of art which cut themselves off from everyday life. They, too, appear like things in themselves, quite divorced from the history that gives birth to them. Like Leverkühn himself, they stand free of their social surroundings. Like good and evil, they seem to be self-born.

There are other affinities between evil and Adrian's art. Both, for example, involve a certain coterie-mindedness. We have seen in the case of Pinkie that evil is a highly exclusive affair, a club to which only a spiritual elect may apply, and the damnably proud Leverkühn is another case in point. For him, ordinary life is paltry and degraded. Moreover, just as evil is nihilistic, so too in a sense is the kind of avant-garde art Adrian produces. Its aim is to obliterate everything that has happened so far and start again from scratch. Only by blowing up its predecessors can it present itself as original. The devil, who puts in a guest appearance in *Doctor Faustus,* turns out to be a revolutionary avant-gardist himself, a sort of Rimbaud or Schoenberg with a cloven hoof. He despises middle-class mediocrity (it has, he scoffs, "no theological status"), and recommends despair as the true path to redemption. God is interested in saints and sinners, not in boringly well-behaved suburbanites. Extremes meet: at least those in despair are capable of spiritual depth, and are thus botched or parodic versions of the saints. Whatever else one might say of the devil, he has a robust contempt for the straitlaced middle classes. In this sense, he resembles the shaggy-haired Bohemian artist. But the Nazis despised suburban morality as well.

Besides, everyday existence has grown so alienated and banal that only a dose of the diabolical can stir it up. When life grows stale and insipid, art may find itself being forced to sup with the devil, raiding the extreme and unspeakable in order to make an effect. It must transgress outworn conventions in its snarling, iconoclastic, Satanic way. It needs to summon the resources of the exotic and extreme. A demoniac art sets out to smash our suburban complacency and release our repressed energies. In this way, perhaps, some good might finally be salvaged from evil. From Charles Baudelaire to Jean Genet, the artist is complicit with the criminal, madman, devil-worshipper, and subversive. This conveniently overlooks the fact that some modernist art is as empty in its own way as the suburban existence it scorns. In its hankering for pure form, it is ravished by a vision of non-being.

Behind these artistic issues in *Doctor Faustus* lies a deeper political question. Fascism must be resisted, but are conventional liberalism and humanism really up to the task? Isn't liberalism as much a spineless doctrine as an honourable one? How can a creed which turns its eyes in civilised distaste from what is truly diabolical in humanity hope to vanquish it? Perhaps, then, in a homeopathic kind of gesture, we should embrace the demonic in order to defeat it. Socialism and modernism may both be perilous options, but at least they cut to the same depth as fascism itself, which is more than can be said for liberal humanism. Mann's liberal-humanist narrator in the novel is far too decent, reasonable a soul to take the full, monstrous measure of what he is confronting. Modernist art from Baudelaire to Yeats has a brisk way with such urbane enlightenment. Instead, it proclaims that only by descending into hell, confronting the savage, irrational, and obscene in humanity, is redemption conceivable. Socialism, rather similarly, holds that only through solidarity with those who are written off as scum of the earth, with the dangerous and dispossessed, can history be transformed. Freudianism has the foolhardy courage to stare the Medusa's head of the unconscious full in the face. Yet does this not then align these creeds with the very barbarism they are out to overcome? Can one really sup with the devil like this and slink off without being poisoned? Should one clear away the rubble of liberal humanism to create the space for a better world, or does such clearing simply pave the way for the emergence of some frightful rough beast?

In the end, perhaps, it all comes down to one's stance toward death. You can disavow death as an intolerable affront to the living, in the manner of Mann's humanist narrator. Or, like his friend Leverkühn, you can clasp it to your bosom for all the wrong reasons. Adrian courts death, in the form of venereal disease, in order to reap from it a kind of hectic half-life, a debauched pastiche of genuine existence. He exists as a kind of self-vampire or self-parasite, sucking life from his own steady dissolution, languishing in some twilight region between the living and the dead. This is a condition commonly associated with evil. Of all the icons associated with the condition, the vampire is the most revealing—for evil, as we shall see, is about leeching life from others in order to fill an aching absence in oneself. The uncanniness we feel in the presence of a doll that seems sinisterly alive is a dim echo of this situation. Art, too, is suspended between life and death. The work of art seems full of vital energy, but it is no more than an inanimate object. The mystery of art is how black marks on a page, or pigment on a canvas, or the scraping of a bow on catgut, can be so richly evocative of life.

Experimental art like Adrian's also embraces death in the shape of the "inhumanity" of artistic form. Rather than being crammed with sensuous content, Leverkühn's music is austerely impersonal. Form is the nonhuman dimension of art, which is one reason why a warm-blooded realism tries to conceal it. Yet if Adrian's art is clinical and analytic in the extreme, it is also exactly the reverse. In its diabolical energies, it represents a retreat from the top-heavy intellectuality of the modern age to the primitive and spontaneous. A good deal of modernist art seeks to achieve a fusion between the archaic and the avant-garde. T. S. Eliot's *The Waste Land* might stand as an example. The true artist, Eliot once remarked, must be both more primitive and more sophisticated than his or her fellow citizens. If civilisation is to be replenished, you must draw on the primeval energies of the past. But this unholy coupling of the very new and the very old is also true of Nazism, which in this sense is a typically modernist phenomenon. On the one hand, Nazism marches ecstatically toward a revolutionary future, trundling behind it the latest gleaming technologies of death. On the other hand, it is a question of blood, earth, instinct, mythology, and the dark gods. This combination is one reason for its potent appeal. It would seem that there is nobody fascism cannot seduce, from mystics to mechanical engineers, bright-eyed champions of progress to stuffed-shirt reactionaries.

Both modernism and fascism, then, seek to unite the primitive and the progressive. Their aim is to mix sophistication with spontaneity, civilisation with Nature, the intelligentsia with the People. The technological drive of the modern must be powered by the "barbarous" instincts of the premodern. We must throw off a rationalistic social order and recapture something of the spontaneity of the "savage." But this is no simple-minded return to Nature. On the contrary, as Adrian Leverkühn argues in his Nietzschean fashion, the new barbarism will be self-conscious, unlike the old. It will represent a kind of higher, cerebral version of the old "savagery," one that raises it to the level of the modern analytical mind. So it is that a sophisticated reason, and all the elemental forces that it has repressed, can be united once again. It is the kind of ethic that Rupert Birkin, the hero of D. H. Lawrence's *Women in Love,* finds so repugnant in the self-consciously "decadent" upper-class types around him. An intellectual cult of violence seems even more squalid than the real thing.

How is all this relevant to the subject of evil? It is, one might claim, a false solution to a problem which evil poses. The curious thing about evil is that it seems to be both clinical and chaotic. It has something of Leverkühn's chilly, sardonic rationalism, but delights at the same time in the depraved and orgiastic. Adrian is not just an alienated intellectual. His music also revels in a kind of obscene meaninglessness. It betrays what the narrator calls "both blood-boltered barbarism and bloodless intellectuality." "The proudest intellectuality," he comments, "stands in the most immediate relation to the animal, to naked instinct, is given over most shamelessly to it." How are we to understand this deadly combination?

There is, in fact, no mystery to it at all. Once reason comes unstuck from the senses, the effect on them both is catastrophic. Reason grows abstract and involuted, losing touch with creaturely life. As a result, it can come to regard that life as mere pointless matter to be manipulated. At the same time, the life of the senses tends to run riot, since it is no longer shaped by reason from inside. Once reason stiffens into rationalism, the life of the instincts lapses into sensationalism. Reason becomes a form of meaning void of life, while bodily existence becomes a life sucked dry of sense. If the devil is a supercilious intellectual, he is also a vulgar little clown who mocks the very idea of sense-making. Both nihilist and buffoon are allergic to the slightest whiff of significance. It is no surprise, then, that Adrian's music is obsessed with order yet haunted by a hellish sense of chaos. It is, after all, a familiar fact that those who cling neurotically to order do so often enough to keep some inner turmoil at bay. Christian fundamentalists—stiff-necked types who never stop thinking about sex—are one such example.

The novelist Milan Kundera writes in *The Book of Laughter and Forgetting* of what he calls the "angelic" and "demonic" states of humanity. By "angelic," he means vacuous, grandiloquent ideals which lack a root in reality. The demonic, by contrast, is a cackle of derisive laughter at the very idea that anything human could conceivably have meaning or value. The angelic is too stuffed with meaning, while the demonic is too devoid of it. The angelic consists of high-sounding clichés like "God bless this wonderful country of ours," to which the demonic replies "Yeah, whatever." "If there is too much uncontested meaning on earth (the reign of the angels)," writes Kundera, "man collapses under the burden; if the world loses all meaning (the reign of the demons), life is every bit as impossible." When the devil gave a burst of defiant laughter before God, an angel shouted in protest. The devil's laughter, Kundera comments, "pointed up the meaninglessness of things, the angel's shout rejoiced in how rationally organised, well conceived, beautiful, good, and sensible everything on the earth was." The angelic are like politicians, incurably upbeat and starry-eyed: progress is being made, challenges are being met, quotas are being fulfilled, and God still has a soft spot in his heart for Texas. The demonic, by contrast, are natural-born scoffers and cynics, whose language is closer to what politicians murmur in private than to what they maintain in public. They believe in power, appetite, self-interest, rational calculation, and nothing else. The United States, unusually among nations, is angelic and demonic at the same time. Few other nations combine such high-flown public rhetoric with that meaningless flow of matter known as consumer capitalism. The role of the former is to provide some legitimation for the latter.

Rather as Satan combines angel and demon in his own person, so evil itself unites these two conditions. One side of it—the angelic, ascetic side—wants to rise above the degraded sphere of fleshliness in pursuit of the infinite. But this withdrawal of the mind from reality has the effect of striking the world empty of value. It reduces it to so much meaningless stuff, in which the demonic side of evil can then wallow. Evil always posits either too much or too little meaning—or rather it does both at the same time. This dual face of evil is obvious enough in the case of the Nazis. If they were full of "angelic" bombast about sacrifice, heroism, and purity of blood, they were also in the grip of what Freudians have called "obscene enjoyment," in love with death and non-being. Nazism is a form of crazed idealism which is terrified of human fleshliness. But it is also one long jeering belch in the face of all such ideals. It is both too solemn and too sardonic—full of stiff-gestured bombast about *Führer* and Fatherland, yet cynical to its core.

These two faces of evil are closely linked. The more reason is dissociated from the body, the more the body disintegrates into a meaningless mess of sensation. The more abstracted reason becomes, the less men and women are able to live a meaningful creaturely life. So the more they must resort to mindless sensation to prove to themselves that they still exist. The orgy is the other side of the oratorio. Indeed, Adrian's great oratorio combines the two faces of evil, revealing what the narrator calls "the substantial identity of the most blest with the most accursed, the inner unity of the chorus of child angels and the hellish laughter of the damned." Leverkühn may be a high-minded artist, but he also has an irrepressible impulse "to laugh, most damnably, at the most mysterious and impressive phenomena." This is because reality itself seems to him to be bogus, like a poor imitation or a feeble joke. "Why does everything seem to me like its own parody?" he inquires. He has a keen eye for the fatuous and absurd, which he is able to find absolutely anywhere. Hell is not only atrocious agony. It is torment laced with manic laughter. It is the sneering cackle of those who believe that they have seen through everything, yet who perversely rejoice in the gimcrack, kitschy nature of it all, like intellectuals who feel a horrible fascination for *Big Brother*. Knowing that value is phony is a source of anguish. Yet it also confirms your own spiritual superiority. So your torment is also your delight.

As the devil himself observes of his native region:

True it is that inside these echoless walls it gets right loud, measureless loud, and by much over-filling the ear with screeching and beseeching, gur-gling and groaning, with yauling and bauling and caterwauling, with horrid winding and grinding and racking ecstasies of anguish no man can hear his own tune . . . And therewith mockery and the extreme of ignominy such as belongs with martyr-dom; for this bliss of hell is like a deep-voiced pitiful jeering and scorn of all the immeasurable anguish; it is accompanied by whinnying laughter and the pointing finger; whence the doctrine that the damned have not only torment but mockery and shame to bear; yea, that hell is to be defined as a monstrous combination of suffering and deri-sion, unendurable yet to be endured world with-out end.

The underworld can only be described in a series of self-contradictory phrases: "ecstasies of anguish," "pitiful jeering," "bliss of hell," and so on. It is the ultimate case of *jouissance,* or obscene enjoyment. It vibrates with the masochistic pleasure we reap from being chastised. Hell is as full of masochists as an S-M convention. Being in this infernal hole is a matter of falling under the sovereignty of the death drive, which per-suades us to reap a perverse gratification from our own destruction. The sniggering and buffoonery of the damned signify the mockery of those who know that everything, not least themselves, is entirely futile. There is a twisted sort of satisfaction in being freed from the burden of meaningfulness. It can be heard in the laughter which greets a sermon suddenly punctuated by a belch. Hell is the final victory of nihilism over idealism. It resounds with the hoots and guffaws of those who feel a warped kind of relief because they can fall no further. It is also the manic cackling of those who exult in what seems to be the final secret, one which the wisest are the least likely to stumble upon: that nothing means anything. It is the bellowing of low farce, not the chuckling of high comedy.

Hell is the kingdom of the mad, absurd, monstrous, traumatic, surreal, disgusting and excremental which Jacques Lacan, after the ancient god of havoc, calls *Ate*. It is a landscape of desolation and despair. But it is a despair that its inhabitants would not wish for a moment to be snatched from them. For it is not only what gives them an edge over credulous idealists of every stripe; it is also the misery that assures them that they still exist. Even this, did they but know it, is a lie, for theologically speaking, as we have seen, there can be no life outside God. Like Pincher Martin, the evil, who believe that they have seen through it all, are thus ensnared in illusion to the end.

CHAPTER TWO

Obscene Enjoyment

Some twenty years ago, I published a small study of Shakespeare in which I argued rather rashly that the three witches were the heroines of *Macbeth*.[1] It is an opinion I would still defend, even though Shakespeare himself might well have been bemused by it. But it needs to be modified somewhat in the light of what has been said so far.

What is the evidence for this perverse claim? The three witches of the play are hostile to the violent, hierarchical social order of Macbeth's Scotland, and wreak untold mischief within it. They are exiles from that status-obsessed regime, inhabiting their own sisterly community on its shadowy borderlands.

They have no truck with the established social order of male rivalries and military honours, other than to throw an enormous spanner in its works. Whereas the leading male characters of the drama are intent on jostling for promotion and securing their status, the witches represent a kind of fluidity (they vanish and rematerialise) that undermines all such well-founded identity. As "imperfect speakers" trading in treacherous riddles, they signify a realm of nonmeaning and poetic wordplay on the edges of orthodox society. As the play unfolds, their riddles, or "paltering in a double sense," come to infiltrate the social order itself, breeding ambiguity, spreading havoc, and bringing two royal patriarchs to grief. The sisters tell Macbeth, for example, that he will never be killed by "one of woman born." In fact, he is slain by a man who was delivered by Caesarean section.

In this sense, these hairy harridans represent what one might risk calling the play's unconscious, the place where meanings slither and tangle. In their presence, clear definitions dissolve and oppositions are inverted: fair is foul and foul is fair, nothing is but what is not. The three weird sisters are androgynous (bearded women), and both singular and plural (three-in-one). As such, they strike at the root of all social and sexual stability. They are radical separatists who scorn male power, laying bare the hollow sound and fury at its heart. They are devotees of female cult, whose words and bodies mock rigorous boundaries and make sport of fixed identities. There is, in short, no doubt that these loathsome old hags have been reading all the latest feminist theory to emerge from Paris.

My earlier enthusiasm for these lean-fingered old crones, however, needs to be qualified in one vital respect. The negativity of the witches, who garble definitions and perform "a deed without a name," is indeed a threat to a rigid social order like Macbeth's Scotland. But it is also a threat to any conceivable social order. These toothless old hexes are the enemies of political society as such. Their negativity is one which finds positive existence itself abhorrent, not just the positive existence of bloodstained Scottish noblemen. This is why it can provide no political alterative to these military butchers. In fact, the sisters find an obscene delight in dismembering creaturely life, throwing poisoned entrails, a baby's finger, a newt's eye, a dog's tongue, and a lizard's leg into the revolting brew bubbling in their cauldron.

The witches themselves are distinctly un-animal. They seem to be unconstrained by their bodies, materialising and evaporating at will. In this lack of bodily existence they resemble the Shakespearian Fool, who like them is a kind of shape-changer, and who also speaks a kind of truth in his riddling way. But disembodiment, as with Ariel of *The Tempest,* is a mixed sort of blessing. It is at best a negative sort of freedom. Once Ariel is granted his liberty he evaporates. We have seen already that characters like Pincher Martin and Adrian Leverkühn are dissociated from their own bodies. This disdain for the finite and material, one suspects, may be true of the witches as well.

What makes these snake-eating androgynes so revolutionary, then—the fact that they seem out to subvert political society as such—also suggests what is amiss with them. They can reject the social order as a whole because they reject creaturely existence as a whole. It is simply not the kind of world they inhabit, even if they intersect with it from time to time. And such a refusal of creaturely things, as we have seen, is traditionally associated with evil. A blanket refusal of being means a denial not only of male hierarchies, but of difference and diversity. In the night of the *Macbeth* witches, all cows look black. There is a good way of undermining jealously guarded identities, by bringing warring male aristocrats to grief. But there is also a bad way of doing so, which merges everything into everything else and denies all difference.

Evil is associated with slime because it is featureless and amorphous. In Robert Louis Stevenson's fable *The Strange Case of Dr. Jekyll and Mr. Hyde,* Jekyll thinks of the evil Hyde, "for all his energy of life, as of something not only hellish but inorganic. This was the shocking thing: that the slime of the pit seemed to utter cries and voices; that what was dead and had no shape, should usurp the offices of life."[2] Evil has the sameness of shit, or the sameness of bodies in a concentration camp. It is like the thick gruel into which the three sisters casually toss everything from a dog's tongue to a stillborn baby's finger. One face of evil may be elitist, but the other is just the opposite. Created things are too trivial to be worth distinguishing between. The innocent as well as the guilty in *Macbeth* are torn apart by the deadly process the witches initiate. There is not much to celebrate in that.

There is another sense in which one should be sceptical of the sisters. Being outside political society, they have no aims or ambitions; and this lack of concern for tomorrow is reflected in the fact that they live in cyclical rather than linear time. Time for the witches goes in circles rather than moves forward in a straight line, as it does, futilely, for Macbeth ("Tomorrow and tomorrow and tomorrow . . ."). Linear time is the medium of aspiration and achievement—whereas these duplicitous hags are associated with dancing in a circle, the cycles of the moon, and verbal repetition. They also bend time by their prophetic prevision. For them, the future has already happened. When their negativity infects Macbeth, however, it takes the form of a desire stretching endlessly into the future. This is because humans, unlike witches, live in time. Negativity becomes a form of "vaulting ambition" which can never rest content with the present, but must continually annul it in its eagerness for the next achievement. In this play, each step such a desire takes to consolidate itself unravels it a little further. Macbeth ends up chasing a secure identity which continually eludes him. Desire undoes itself as it goes along. Actions taken to armour-plate Macbeth's regal status result in upending it. So when the nothingness of the witches enters into human history, it becomes purely destructive. It shows up as the hollow at the heart of desire, which drives it on to yet more flawed, fruitless achievement. There is, as we have seen, a good and a bad kind of nothingness; and the ghastly gorgons of this play might be said to combine the two.

Why do these skinny-fingered harpies want to bring low Duncan, Macbeth, Banquo, Macduff's family, and various other characters in the first place? The play itself ventures no opinion. It yields no answer because there is none. The witches' deadly deceptions are entirely pointless. They have no particular end in sight, any more than do their circular dances around the cauldron. The sisters are not out to achieve anything, since achievement is part of the society they repudiate. Achievement belongs to the realm of means and ends, causes and effects; and this realm is alien to these filth-dabbling feminists. They are sorceresses, not strategists. They seek to destroy Macbeth not because he is black-hearted (in fact, he is not until he encounters them), but simply for the hell of it.

Here, then, we arrive at an insight which seems central to the idea of evil. It has, or appears to have, no practical purpose. Evil is supremely pointless. Anything as humdrum as a purpose would tarnish its lethal purity. In this, it resembles God, who if he does turn out to exist has absolutely no reason for doing so. He is his own reason for being. He also created the universe just for fun, not for some purpose. Evil rejects the logic of causality. If it were to have an end in view, it would be self-divided, non-self-identical, out ahead of itself.

But nothingness cannot be carved up in this fashion. This is why it cannot really exist in time. For time is a matter of difference, whereas evil is boringly, perpetually, the same. It is in this sense that hell is said to be for all eternity.

The other great Shakespearian example of an evil which seems to lack all purpose is Iago in *Othello*. Iago offers various motives for his aversion to the Moor, just as Shylock does for his antipathy to Antonio in *The Merchant of Venice*. In both cases, however, the stated reasons seem oddly unequal to the virulence of the hatred. Both men also offer a suspicious surplus of motives, as though they are trying to rationalise a passion which they themselves cannot quite fathom. It is tempting, then, to find the root of Iago's hostility to Othello in his nihilism. Iago is a cynic and materialist who believes in nothing but will and appetite, and who regards all objective value as worthless: "Virtue? A fig! 'Tis in ourselves that we are thus or thus. Our bodies are our gardens to the which our wills are the gardeners; so that if we will plant nettles or sow lettuce, set hyssop and weed up thyme . . . why, the power and corrigible authority of this lies in our wills."

The world is mere pliable stuff, which the all-sovereign individual will can shape however it pleases. And this also applies to oneself. Human beings are self-fashioning, self-creating creatures. They take their cue from themselves rather than from God, Nature, human kinship, or objective value. Several of Shakespeare's notorious villains champion this case. They are naturalists or anticonventionalists through and through. Values, images, ideals, and conventions are just so much window dressing or icing on the cake, which the wicked claim to have seen right through. In fact, to imagine that there could be a human reality without these dimensions is to be even more naive than the credulous Othello. Those who seek to be authors of themselves are rather like the state of sexual jealousy, which, as Iago's wife Emilia observes in this play, is "a monster, / Begot upon itself, born on itself." There is something peculiarly pointless and malevolent in Shakespeare's mind about things that bring themselves to birth, feed upon themselves, or define themselves tautologically in their own terms. It is an image to which he returns in his drama again and again. Coriolanus is an example of this idle circularity—a character who behaves "as if a man were author of himself / And knew no other kin." But this proud singularity is also pure vacuity: "He was a kind of nothing, titleless, / Till he had forg'd himself a name i' the fire / Of burning Rome."

Iago, like many a Shakespearian cynic, is partly a clown, reveling as he does in debunking and deflating. Hannah Arendt remarks of the Nazi executive of genocide Adolf Eichmann that "everyone (at his trial) could see that this man was not a 'monster,' but it was difficult indeed not to suspect that he was a clown."[3] Eichmann, she thinks, was not a diabolical character who consciously adopted evil as his good. Nor was he a grand figure of evil like Macbeth, or even just plain stupid. It was "sheer thoughtlessness," Arendt considers, that made him one of the greatest of modern criminals. Audaciously, she finds something not only banal in this but "even funny."[4] Yet when clowning is pushed to the point of denying all value, it indeed becomes monstrous. Farce is human actions stripped of meaning and reduced to mere physical motion. This is also what the Nazis had in mind for the Jews.

Debunkery, to be sure, can be a positive kind of foolery. It punctures the pompous delusions of the self-deceived. But it can also sail perilously close to the nihilism of those like Iago, who can win a vicarious kind of identity for themselves only by deriding and destroying. There is always a touch of bathos about this kind of evil, which takes a malicious delight in hacking things down to size. The problem, then, is that a healthy iconoclasm can sail very close to a pathological cynicism. Iago has only to clap eyes on virtue and beauty to feel the intolerable itch to deface it. Something of his attitude to Othello is captured in what he comments of another character, Cassio: "He hath a daily beauty in his life / That makes me ugly."

In contrast with Iago, Othello seems enraptured by the integrity of his own being. There is an air of monumental self-satisfaction about him which irritates Iago beyond endurance. His self-admiration is reflected in his rotund, oratorical speech:

> Like to the Pontic sea,
> Whose icy current and compulsive course
> N'er feels retiring ebb, but keeps due on

To the Propontic and the Hellespont;
Even so my bloody thoughts, with violent pace,
Shall n'er look back, 'n'er ebb to humble love,
Till that a capable and wide revenge
Swallow them up.

This is the kind of thing that makes the streetwise Iago squirm. He can see such exalted idealism only as bogus, which perhaps in part it is. In Milan Kundera's terms, then, Othello is angelic whereas Iago is demonic. Othello's language is too stuffed with mouth-filling rhetoric, too extravagant and hyperbolic. Iago's speech, by contrast, is coarse and pragmatic. Like a number of other Shakespearian villains, his attitude to language is strictly functional. He speaks scoffingly of the Moor's discourse as "a bombast circumstance / Horribly stuffed with epithets of war." For all its malicious intent, this is not a bad description of a hero who can toss off phrases like "exsufflicate and blown surmises." Even Othello's final suicide, which he prefaces with a typically sonorous set speech, is what one critic has called "a magnificent *coup de théâtre*," delivered with one canny eye on the audience. This military hero seems to live straight out of an inflated image of himself. Because his identity is so wholly externalised, it leaves a kind of absence or vacuum behind it, which his enemy can then move in on.

From Iago's viewpoint, Othello represents a pompous

plenitude of being which conceals an inner lack. And this lack, ironically, is his inability to see that there is anything lacking in his identity—anything unstable or incomplete about it. His exalted sense of himself is a way of not having to confront the chaos of his inner being. Iago, by contrast, remarks of himself that "I am not what I am"—meaning that while Othello seems more or less identical with his public image as a warrior, his own selfhood is just an empty excess over whatever mask he presents to the world at any given moment. Iago can be defined only in negative terms, as the other of whatever he appears to be. The same goes for his comment that "I am nothing if not critical." Like a critic, he is parasitic on creation—a creation he secretly despises. Lacking any sturdy identity himself—he is an *actor*, a purely performative figure—he lives only in the act of subverting the selfhood of others.

So it is that Iago, goaded beyond endurance by Othello's apparently seamless selfhood, sets out to dismantle it. He begins this demolition process by insinuating an insidious nothing into the heart of the Moor's identity. Whereas in *Macbeth* this insidious nothing takes the form of political ambition, in *Othello* it takes the form of sexual jealousy. Othello asks Iago what is troubling him, to which Iago replies, "Nothing, my lord." Ironically, this response is exact. There is, indeed, nothing ailing him at all. But Iago rightly speculates that Othello will promptly read some dreadful something—

the supposed infidelity of his wife Desdemona—into this modest disclaimer. The negativity which will gnaw away at Othello is the nothingness of groundless sexual jealousy.

Like the paltering of the *Macbeth* witches, this nameless dread undermines all stability of selfhood. It converts the whole world into a terrifying state of ambiguity. Contradiction, inversion, doubleness, and garbled logic are the marks of this condition, as they are of the *Macbeth* witches. "I think my wife be honest," Othello groans, "and think she is not." He is pitched by Iago's crafty suggestions into that distraught state of mind in which one can believe and disbelieve the same thing at the same time. In his paranoid jealousy, the world becomes a text which can be endlessly interpreted and misinterpreted. One can read the most hideous of senses into its apparently innocuous signs. Othello is bent on plucking out the heart of the mystery, oblivious of the fact that there is no mystery at all. Everything around him appears sinisterly unreal, since it is all just a painted show which refuses to speak of the dreadful sexual reality it is masking. Nothing is but what is not. The pathologically jealous cannot accept the scandal that everything lies open to view, that things are simply the way they are, that what one is seeing is, would you believe it, the real thing. As the paranoically jealous Leontes cries in *The Winter's Tale:*

Is whispering nothing?
Is leaning cheek to cheek? Is meeting noses?

Kissing with inside lip? . . .
Why, then the world and all that's in't is nothing;
The covering sky is nothing; Bohemia nothing;
My wife is nothing; nor nothing have these
    nothings
If this be nothing . . .

Everywhere you look you see nothing, rather like Pincher Martin as the rock, sky, and ocean dissolve. Language, like Iago's "Nothing," tears a gaping hole in the world. It makes absent things present, inducing you to see with intolerable clarity what is not there at all.

Othello is particularly prey to this delusion, since in Freudian terms he has sublimated his "lower" drives into an exalted idealism. Those who do this, according to Freud, weaken those instincts, and in doing so leave them prey to the death drive. This is why the angelic can capsize without warning into the demonic, as Othello is reduced in a mere handful of scenes from a revered public icon to a gibbering, sex-crazed maniac. His stately eloquence falls steadily apart at the seams, as he greets a group of visiting dignitaries with the demented cry, "Goats and monkeys!" It is not quite the sort of welcome one expects from a high-ranking state official. The idealised Desdemona has acted for him as a kind of fetish—the function of the fetish, for Freud, being to block out the turbulent realities of the unconscious. "O I do love her," Othello moans, "and when I love her not / Chaos is come again." If he needs his wife's love, it is largely to block off a terrifying insight into himself. And it is by working on this absence from himself that Iago can induce his identity to implode.

There are many literary works about evil, but not many of them have been condemned as evil themselves. This, however, was the fate of Pierre de Laclos's *Les Liaisons Dangereuses* (1782), which some young ladies of the time would read only behind locked doors, and which was eventually condemned as "dangerous" by the royal court of Paris. The protagonists of the book, the Marquise de Merteuil and her ex-lover the Vicomte de Valmont, are monsters of manipulation who bring others to ruin through sexual intrigue largely for the sake of the sport. Valmont coldbloodedly sets out to seduce the saintly Présidente de Torvel, since her piety and chastity make her an "enemy" worthy of his machinations. In this sense, there is a touch of Iago in his attitude to her. Having taken half the novel to seduce the pious Présidente, he casts her off and leaves her to die in despair. He then revenges himself on Madame de Volanges, who had tried to warn the Présidente de Torvel of his unsavoury character, by seducing her fifteen-year-old daughter, Cécile. He is particularly amused by imagining what her respectable fiancé will make on their wedding night of the sophisticated sexual techniques in which he has groomed her. Cécile ends up pregnant and retires to a convent; the outraged young nobleman who loves her kills Valmont in a duel.

Valmont's enthusiastic partner-in-crime is the Marquise

de Merteuil, a woman with a claim to be one of the most black-hearted scoundrels of world literature. The two debauched aristocrats are connoisseurs of the art of "love," a game which they conduct with all the sadistic delectation of psychopaths. In this dissipated Parisian high society, one's lover is one's antagonist, to court her is to hunt her to the kill, and to bed her is to destroy her. Valmont and his former mistress are not wicked because they are the victims of uncontrollable passion, but precisely because they are not. It is their fusion of the cerebral and the erotic which marks them out as so stereotypically Gallic. This patrician pair are as dissociated from their own emotional life as Adrian Leverkühn, which is why they lay waste to the vulnerable creatures around them. Love is a military skirmish or psychological experiment, to be conducted for the sheer destructive relish of it. It has almost nothing to do with affection. In this malign lack of motive for their conquests, the two come very close to a traditional kind of evil. It is a condition which can be found all the way from Sade to Sartre. There is good reason to believe that the devil is a Frenchman.

Othello presents us with the spectacle of one man systematically destroying another, and for no apparent reason. Evil, it would seem, is an example of pure disinterestedness. If this is true, then the surprising fact is that scarcely any of the literary figures we have examined so far qualify for the title. Golding's Pincher Martin, on the evidence the novel yields us, does not exterminate others for the hell of it. On the contrary, he is not the kind of man to do anything for its own sake, whether creative or destructive. It is hard to imagine him whistling cheerfully away at the potter's wheel. Martin's will serves his ruthless self-interest—whereas "pure" evil ravages and exterminates even when this threatens to sabotage the interests of those in the grip of it. In fact, it can cause them a fair amount of anguish, as we shall see shortly. It is just that, for the evil, this anguish is also a source of keen gratification. As the philosopher John Rawls writes (rather surprisingly, for those acquainted with his usual dryly academic tones), "What moves the evil man is the love of injustice: he delights in the impotence and humiliation of those subject to him and relishes being recognised by them as the author of their degradation."[5] Evil is pure perversity. It is a kind of cosmic cross-grainedness. It may claim to invert conventional moral values, so that injustice becomes an accomplishment to be admired; but it secretly believes in none of them.

Graham Greene's Pinkie betrays some of the traditional features of evil. But he, too, kills for practical reasons (to avoid being identified as a criminal, for example), not for its own sake. In this, he resembles gangsters in general, who are not generally given to what the French know as an *acte gratuit*, or deliberately pointless action. Thomas Mann's Adrian Leverkühn destroys nobody but himself, even if he holds himself responsible for the death of a child. Nor does he do away with himself just for the hell of it. There is an artistic purpose to his prolonged suicide. The nameless narrator of *The Third Policeman* is certainly in hell; but he murders old Mathers for financial gain, not as an end in itself. So perhaps what one might call the merely vicious end up in hell, too, alongside the positively evil. The *Macbeth* witches appear to lay waste to human life purely for the sake of it, but we have seen that, like real-life witches, they are by no means as black as the critics have painted them. Perhaps Iago fills the bill with the fewest qualifications.

It might be argued that any definition of evil which excludes such a rogues' gallery is self-defeatingly narrow. Isn't such a sense of evil too technical and precise for its own good? It defines evil, in effect, as what Immanuel Kant calls "radical" evil. It sees it as willing wickedness for wickedness's sake, which Kant did not in fact think was possible. For him, even the most depraved of individuals must acknowledge the authority of the moral law. But the tightness of the definition might also suggest how extraordinarily rare evil actually is, despite those who slap the label cavalierly on toddler killers or North Korea. There are also dangers in too broad a definition of the term. Kant, for example, uses terms like evil, wickedness, depravity, and corruption of behaviour which most laidback liberals would count as no more than mildly immoral. For him, evil lies in our propensity to deviate from the moral law. But evil is a lot more interesting than that. And not all such deviations are worthy of the name.

Perhaps evil is not all that rare in the upper echelons of fascist organisations. But fascist organisations are themselves gratifyingly thin on the ground, at least most of the time. It is true that when evil does break out, it tends to do so, like air crashes, in a big way. The Holocaust springs instantly to mind. Even so, we should keep in mind what an exceptional event the Holocaust was. It was not of course exceptional in involving the murder of vast numbers of innocent men, women, and children. The state butcheries of Stalin and Mao disposed of many more individuals. The Holocaust was unusual because the rationality of modern political states is in general an instrumental one, geared to the achievement of specific ends. It is astonishing, then, to find a kind of monstrous *acte gratuit,* a genocide for the sake of genocide, an orgy of extermination apparently for the hell of it, in the midst of the modern era. Such evil is almost always confined to the private sphere. The so-called Moors murderers of 1960s Britain, who do not appear to have been mad, and who seem to have tortured and killed children just for the obscene pleasure of it, might furnish an example.

By contrast, instances of public devastation for its own sake are exceedingly hard to come by. For one thing, such events require an enormous amount of organising; and people are naturally reluctant to devote time and energy to such enterprises unless they can see a substantial payoff. Mass psychosis is scarcely an everyday occurrence, unless one were to include religion or the Michael Jackson fan club under that heading. One of the most grotesque features of the Nazi death camps was the way in which sober, meticulous, utilitarian measures were pressed into the service of an operation which had no practical point at all. It is as though individual bits and piece of the project made sense, but not the overall operation. The same is true of a game, in which purposive moves are made within a situation which has no practical function.

Stalin and Mao massacred for a reason. For the most part, there was a brutal kind of rationality behind their murders. This does not render their actions less heinous or culpable than those of the Nazis. The victims of such enormities, after all, are not especially bothered about whether they perish for no particular reason or in accordance with some meticulous plan. In fact, crimes committed with an end in view can be more reprehensible than those perpetrated with no apparent motive. Throwing a complete stranger out of a railway carriage just for the hell of it, as happens in André Gide's novel *Les Caves du Vatican*, is not as bad as throwing out half a dozen strangers in order to create more elbow room for yourself. The crimes of Stalin and Mao are not necessarily less abominable than those of Hitler. They are just in a different category.

Some would claim that the so-called Final Solution was not in fact without purpose. After all, if it was seen by the Nazis as a solution, then it presumably had some point. For one thing, demonising Jews served the cause of national unity, which is always easier to achieve in the face of an omnipresent danger. There were also clear, practical reasons for disposing of political enemies of the regime, like Communists. For another thing, murdering sexual "perverts" or the mentally or physically disabled was thought to purify the German race. We shall consider the purification-of-the-race explanation in a moment. It is worth noting, however, that you do not need to kill six million people to manufacture a bogeyman. In any case, people can be scapegoated without being eradicated. In fact, the two ends are ultimately irreconcilable. If you dispose of your scapegoat, you will need to find a substitute. So what, after all, was the Final Solution a solution to?

It is also true that there is sometimes no clear line between the pragmatic and the nonpragmatic. Which category, for example, does the Inquisition fall into? Art and humour are largely nonpragmatic, in the sense that they do not usually have much practical effect. Even so, they are capable of producing such effects every now and then. Think of a patriotic march composed to celebrate the nation's military conquests. Purges and pogroms generally have some political point—to seize land, for example, or to destroy potential enemies of the state. Yet they are rarely reducible to these practical goals, as the excessive violence invested in them might suggest. If they are as savage as they are, it is because they usually involve not just land or power but people's identities. Human beings will often go to quite barbarous lengths to carry on being themselves. In any such campaign, the pragmatic and nonpragmatic are often interwoven. For Sigmund Freud, the death drive is always pointlessly, sadistically in excess of the practical ends to which we harness it (subjugating Nature, for example). It is a notoriously unreliable servant, always in danger of scampering off to do its own thing. Primo Levi remarks how violence during the Hitler epoch always seemed either an end in itself or disproportionate to its purpose.[6]

The Holocaust was not irrational in the sense of being some purely random slaughter, as if one were to murder six million violinists, or six million individuals with hazel-coloured eyes. Those who perished did so because they were Jews or Roma or homosexuals, or some other group of people whom the Nazis considered undesirable. That gay men and women and left-wingers were slaughtered serves to remind us that the Final Solution was not simply a matter of massacring those considered to be ethnic or racial aliens, as Jews (including German Jews) were thought to be. But why were all these people considered undesirable? Because they were thought to pose a threat to the purity and unity of the German nation and the so-called Aryan race. So perhaps this was a sufficient reason for the death camps.

The threat, however, was not for the most part a practical one. By and large, these so-called aliens posed a danger to the state not by what they got up to but simply by virtue of existing, rather as Othello's very existence seems to menace Iago. This is not just because they were "Other," in the fashionable postmodern jargon. Nazi Germany had plenty of "Others," including the Allies; but it did not have well-drafted plans to exterminate them en masse, as opposed to bombing them into the ground. The Nazis did not murder Belgians simply because they were Belgians. The Allies posed a literal danger to the Nazis, but they did not constitute what might be called an ontological threat—a threat to their very being. They did not sap away insidiously at the root of their identity, as Jews and others were thought to do. The kind of others who drive you to mass murder are usually those who for some reason or other have come to signify the terrible non-being at the core of oneself. It is this aching absence which you seek to stuff with fetishes, moral ideals, fantasies of purity, the manic will, the absolute state, the phallic figure of the Führer. In this, Nazism resembles some other brands of fundamentalism. The obscene enjoyment of annihilating the Other becomes the only way of convincing yourself that you still exist. The non-being at the core of one's own identity is, among other things, a foretaste of death; and one way of fending off the terror of human mortality is to liquidate those who incarnate this trauma in their own person. In this way, you demonstrate that you have authority over the only antagonist—death—that cannot be vanquished even in principle.

Power loathes weakness because it rubs its nose in its own secret frailty. Jews for the Nazis were a kind of slimy nothingness or excrescence, an obscene marker of humanity at its most shamefully vulnerable. It was this which had to be annihilated if the Nazis' own integrity of being were to be preserved. For the philosopher Otto Weininger, it is women who embody a kind of frightful nonexistence. Their seduction of men, he argues in *Sex and Character*, represents the infinite craving of Nothing for Something. Yet how do you obliterate nothingness? And how do you know when you have been successful? Isn't it absurdly self-defeating to imagine that you can quell the fear of nothingness inside you by creating even more of the stuff around you? The truth is that non-being cannot be destroyed, which is why the Third Reich would indeed have had to flourish for at least a thousand years, if not for all time. This is also why hell in popular mythology endures for ever and ever. There is always more disgusting material stuff to be eradicated—always a finer, more perfect purity to be attained. To kill every Jew on the planet was an alluring proposition to the Nazis for several reasons, but one of them lay in its aesthetic perfection. There is a diabolical delight to be reaped from the notion of absolute destruction. Flaws, loose ends, and rough approximations are what evil cannot endure. This is one reason why it has a natural affinity with the bureaucratic mind. Goodness, by contrast, is in love with the dappled, unfinished nature of things.

We have seen already, however, how evil presents two different faces here, which the Nazis above all exemplify. On the one hand, it is a kind of insidious deficiency of being; on the other hand, it is just the opposite—a monstrous spawning of meaningless matter. For Nazi ideology, Jews and their fellow victims signified both at the same time. On the one hand, they represented a lack of being—one which, as we have seen, threatened to evoke the Nazis' horror of their own essential nothingness. On the other hand, Jews represented meaningless matter, sheer subhuman garbage. As such, they posed a threat to the "angelic" aspect of Nazism, its rage for order and idealism. However many Jews you slaughtered, however much you insisted on discipline and authority, there would always be some of this human excrement left around to pollute your exalted schemes. As Milan Kundera writes in *The Book of Laughter and Forgetting,* "Death has two faces. One is non-being; the other is the terrifying material being that is the corpse." Death is both a lack of being and an excess of it. It is portentously meaningful, but also as blank as an empty page.

What these two dimensions of evil have in common is a horror of impurity. On the one hand, you can see impurity as the nauseating slime of negativity—in which case purity lies in an angelic fullness of being. On the other hand, impurity can be seen as the obscenely bulging excess of the material world, once it has been stripped of sense and value. Compared to this, it is non-being which signifies purity. The Nazis swung constantly between these two stances. They veered between the angelic and the demonic—between repelling chaos and reveling in it. As far as the latter goes, we have the testimony of the German theologian Karl Jaspers, writing in the shadow of Nazism, who speaks of its "delight in meaningless activity, in torturing and being tortured, in destruction for its own sake, in the raging hatred against the world and man complete with the raging hatred against one's own despised existence."[7] It would be hard to find a more pithy summary of the diabolical. Evil is a conundrum or contradiction, which is one reason why the *Macbeth* witches palter in a double sense. It is austere, but it is also dissolute. It is spiritually elevated but also corrosively cynical. It involves a megalomaniac overvaluing of the self, and an equally pathological devaluing of it.

Let us return, then, to the question of whether evil is best seen as a kind of purposeless or nonpragmatic wickedness. In one sense, the answer is surely yes. Evil is not primarily concerned with practical consequences. As the French psychoanalyst André Green writes, "Evil is without 'why' because its raison d'être is to proclaim that everything which exists has no meaning, obeys no order, pursues no aim, depends only on the power it can exercise to impose its will on the objects of its appetite."[8] It is not a bad description of Pinkie or Pincher Martin. Yet the evil do have purposes of a kind. They may seem to lay waste simply for the hell of it, but this is not the whole truth. We have seen already that they visit violence upon those who pose a threat to their own identity. But they also smash and sabotage to ease the hellish conflict in which they are caught, of which we shall see more in a moment. The evil are in pain, and like a lot of people in pain will go to extreme lengths to find relief. These, then, are reasons of a kind, even if they are not of the same order as butchering peasants for their counterrevolutionary views. In this sense, then, even evil has a grisly kind of rationality about it.

It is true that we can push the question one stage back and ask *why* one should want to cling to one's identity. It is not as though there is always some compelling practical reason to do so. In fact, practically speaking, I might well be better off being someone else. Mick Jagger springs to mind. You might claim, as the Nazis did, that your identity is immeasurably superior to that of others—so that if this master race were to founder, a lot that is precious would go under with it. But it is not hard to see that this is really a way of rationalising the pathological drive to self-identity which the Nazis betrayed. And this, one might argue, was simply a more lurid, lethal version of our own everyday compulsion to persist in what we are.

There is no particular reason why we should want to carry on being Algerians, trapeze artists, or Anglo-Catholic vegans. In fact, there are times when we want to persist in an identity which we do not especially prize. It is simply that the ego has a built-in drive to keep itself intact. One can see, then, why the question of whether evil is functional or not is so ambiguous. Evil is committed in the name of something else, and to this extent has a purpose; but this something else does not itself have a point. Iago destroys Othello partly because he sees him as a monstrous threat to his own identity; but why this should be a good reason for destroying him remains impenetrable. Even so, Iago's actual actions are purposeful enough—which is why it is not quite true to say that evil is done for its own sake. Rather, it is purposeful action taken in the name of a condition which is not itself purposeful. Here again, one of its closest analogies would be a game.

In fact any purposeful activity, if you push it far back

enough, turns out to be in the service of some nonpurposeful state of affairs. Why did she run for the bus? Because she wanted to get to the pharmacist's shop before it closed. Why did she want to do that? To buy some toothpaste. Why did she want some toothpaste? To brush her teeth. Why brush your teeth? To stay healthy. Why stay healthy? So as to carry on enjoying life. But what is so precious about an enjoyable life? It is not a value that Pinkie signs up for. Here, as Ludwig Wittgenstein would say, one's spade hits rock bottom. Reasons, as he remarks in *Philosophical Investigations,* have to come to an end somewhere. Only five-year-olds, with their relentless metaphysical questioning, fail to accept this.

In his study *Ethics, Evil, and Fiction,* the philosopher Colin McGinn points out that the sadist values pain for its own sake, which is why he creates as much of it as he can by inflicting it on other people. The sadist does not regard pain as serving any specific purpose, as sergeant-majors and probably the Duke of Edinburgh tend to do. There are, McGinn considers, kinds of evil which do indeed have a purpose. But there is also a kind of "primitive" evil which is purely unmotivated, and which admits of no further explanation. It is just, so McGinn remarks, that some people are "hooked up" that way. One reason why he needs to resort to this rather feeble phrase is that, as an orthodox Anglo-Saxon philosopher, he will have no truck with such Continental mysteries as psychoanalysis. (The same oversight leads him to some strikingly implausible remedies for combating evil.) If McGinn was prepared to pay those ideas their due, he might see that evil is not just any old kind of sadism. It is the kind of cruelty which seeks to relieve a frightful inner lack. And to this extent even "primitive" evil is not entirely without its motives.

In fact, elsewhere in his book, McGinn comes up with an excellent argument which threatens to undermine his own case about the motivelessness of evil. He points out that the effect of intense suffering is to undermine the value of human existence. For those in agony, life has become an intolerable burden to be shucked off. A lot of people in acute pain would rather be dead. And some of those who are spiritually dead rejoice in witnessing this torment, because it confirms their own ascetic contempt for human existence. So their relish for other people's afflictions has a reason. (In a similar way, being pained by someone else's success [i.e., envy] has a point, since other people's achievements confront us humiliatingly with our own failures.) There is a kind of sadist who makes others howl in order to transform them into part of his own nihilistic nature. Evil brings false comfort to those in anguish by murmuring in their ear that life has no value anyway. Its enemy, as always, is not so much virtue as life itself. If it spits in the face of virtue, it is because, as Aristotle and Aquinas were aware, virtue is by far the fullest, most deeply enjoyable way to live.

In that great monument to human gloom *The World as Will and Idea,* the nineteenth-century philosopher Arthur Schopenhauer distinguished between what he called the good, the bad, and the evil. Bad actions, he thought, were selfish ones; but evil actions did not fall under this heading. They were not just displays of ruthless egoism or fanatical self-interest. By evil, Schopenhauer meant more or less what I have been meaning by the term. He saw evil deeds as motivated by a need to obtain relief from the inner torment of what he called the Will; and this relief was to be gained by inflicting that torment on others. In psychoanalytic terms, evil is thus a form of projection.

The Will, for Schopenhauer, is a malignant drive which lies at the very heart of our being but which is callously indifferent to our personal welfare. It ordains suffering to no end. In fact, it has absolutely no purpose in view other than its own futile self-reproduction. Men and women under the sway of this force, Schopenhauer writes, find one gratification after another wanting, so that "when at last all wishes are exhausted, the pressure of the Will still remains, even without any recognised motive, and makes itself known with terrible pain as a feeling of the most frightful desolation and emptiness."[9] Only when we cease to desire something in particular are we overwhelmed by the sheer painfulness of desire as such, desire in its purest state.

Sigmund Freud, who was much influenced by Schopenhauer, redefined this malignly sadistic force as the death drive. His originality, however, was to argue that we find this vindictive power delightful as well as deadly. There is a sense in which we find death extraordinarily gratifying. *Eros* and *Thanatos*, love and death, are in Freud's view closely interwoven. Both, for example, involve a surrender of the self. Savaged by the superego, ravaged by the id, and battered by the external world, the poor, bruised ego is understandably in love with its own dissolution. Like some badly mutilated beast, it finds that its only final security lies in crawling off to die. Only by returning to the inanimate state from which it set out can it cease to suffer. It is a condition with which literary art has long been familiar. To cease upon the midnight without pain, as Keats writes, is in Hamlet's words a consummation devoutly to be wished. At the end of Thomas Mann's great novel *Buddenbrooks,* the dying Thomas Buddenbrooks comes to realise that "death was a joy, so great, so deep that it could be dreamed of only in moments of revelation like the present. It was the return from an unspeakably painful wandering, the correction of a grave mistake, the loosening of chains, the opening of doors—it put right again a lamentable mischance."

This, then, is the true scandal of psychoanalysis—not infant sexuality, which had been recognized for a long time (not least by infants), but the proposal that human beings unconsciously desire their own destruction. At the core of the self is a drive to absolute nothingness. There is that within us which perversely clamours for our own downfall. To preserve ourselves from the injury known as existing, we are even ready to embrace our own disappearance.

Those who fall under the sway of the death drive feel that ecstatic sense of liberation that springs from the thought that nothing really matters. The delight of the damned is not to give a damn. Even self-interest is set aside—for the damned are in their own twisted way entirely disinterested, eager as they are to bring themselves low along with the rest of creation. The death drive is a deliriously orgiastic revolt against interest, value, meaning, and rationality. It is an insane urge to shatter the lot of them in the name of nothing whatsoever. It has no respect for either the pleasure principle or the reality principle, both of which it is cheerfully prepared to sacrifice for the obscenely gratifying sound of the whole world crashing around its ears.

The death drive is bound up for Freud with the superego, the faculty of moral conscience that rebukes us for our transgressions. In fact, Freud describes the superego as "a pure culture of the death instinct." In punishing us for our transgressions, this reproachful power stokes up in us a lethal culture of guilt. Yet since (masochistic creatures that we are) we also rejoice in the superego's scoldings, we can come to hug our chains, finding a perverse source of pleasure in our very guilt. And this succeeds in making us feel even more guilty. This surplus guilt then brings the high-minded terrorism of the superego down on our heads with even greater vindictive force, with the result that we feel even more guilty, and thus even more gratified, and so on. We are trapped in a vicious circle of guilt and transgression, or Law and desire. The more we try to placate this pitiless Law, the more we are inclined to tear ourselves apart.

At an extreme, this deadlock can plunge us into what Freud calls melancholia, or what we might now call acute clinical depression. And this, at worst, can result in the extinction of the ego by suicide. Every renunciation of instinctual satisfaction strengthens the authority of the superego, reinforces its insane rancour, and so deepens our guilt. This vengeful faculty grows fat on the very desires it forbids. Moreover, in a sourly ironic twist, the Law which punishes our transgressions also provokes them. Without the superego's paranoid prohibitions, we would not be aware of crime and guilt in the first place. As Saint Paul writes in his epistle to the Romans: "If it had not been for the law, I should not have known sin . . . the very commandment which promised life proved to be death to me." This, if you like, is the Freudian version of original sin. For Paul, this vicious circle can be broken only by transforming the Law of censure and condemnation into the Law of love and forgiveness.

Just as Freud argued that dreams were the royal road to the unconscious, so one of our most reliable forms of access to the death drive is addiction. Take, for example, the case of an alcoholic in the throes of a heavy drinking bout. If it is so hard for him to set the bottle aside, it is not because he relishes the taste of the stuff. Indeed, its taste probably leaves him cold. It is because the drink fills some wound or rent in his inner being. In plugging this intolerable gap, it acts as a kind of fetish, as Desdemona does for Othello. But the bottle is also hard to set aside because the alcoholic is addicted to his own destruction. And this is because it is a potent source of pleasure. This is why he continues to drink even when he has shattered every nerve in his body and feels, as they say, like death. The pleasure is inseparable from the self-violence. The death drive is not just content with seeing us tear ourselves to pieces. With boldfaced insolence, it commands us to enjoy the process while we are at it. It wants us to be perverts as well as suicides.

A thief does not break the law for kicks. He does so in order to enrich himself. But when Saint Augustine stole fruit from an orchard as a young man, so he tells us in his *Confessions,* he "took pleasure in the very sin and theft itself . . . I was wicked to no purpose, and there was no cause of this my malice but malice itself. It was deformed, and yet I loved it; I loved to perish. I loved the sin, not that which I obtained by the same; I loved the sin itself . . . not desiring any profit from my shame, but only thirsting after shame itself."[10] Later in the book Augustine writes of those who rejoice in their own wickedness as feeling "a pernicious pleasure and a miserable felicity."[11] It is his way of describing what in our own time has been called obscene enjoyment. The doomed are those who are bound fast to the Law because they are in love with the act of violating it. Each time they kick over the traces, they bring its sadistic fury down on their heads. They do so as surely as an alcoholic squeezes a few last, defiant drops of pleasure from the bottle, in the dreadful knowledge that this will bring upon him the most appalling state of physical and mental collapse.

It is only through this ghastly process that the alcoholic can feel alive—or at least enjoy the kind of wretched twilight existence, suspended between life and death, that the drink yields him. Drinking is the only part of him that is not quite dead, which is why he must cling to it like a drowning man to a plank. If he were to slacken his grip on it for a moment, like Pincher Martin on his rock, then he might have to die for real—which is to say, face the horrifying prospect of having to abandon his addiction and be reborn. It is his dissolution which holds him together. The more he drinks, the more he can act out a grisly parody of being alive; and the longer, therefore, he can stave off the moment when he lapses into agonising pain, as the alcohol ravages his body like Schopenhauer's tormenting Will. As Søren Kierkegaard points out, "As a drunkard keeps himself continually intoxicated from day to day, for fear of stopping and the mental distress that would follow and the possible consequences if he should one day become quite sober, so too with the demonic . . . Only in the continuation of sin does he remain himself."[12]

How much does an alcoholic want to drink? The answer is: an infinite amount. If only his mortal flesh did not get in the way, he would drink all the way from here to eternity. His desire for alcohol is terrifyingly, sublimely inexhaustible. It can survive any number of coronaries, liver transplants, epileptic fits, and frightful hallucinations. Just as for Freud there is something imperishable about the death drive, which like the Nazis will annihilate more and more matter yet still fail to be satiated, so drink for the alcoholic is in no sense a finite entity. Like desire itself, there is always more of it where that came from. And just as desire for psychoanalysis is nothing personal, but rather an anonymous network into which we are inserted at birth, so the drive to destruction is purely formal, utterly impersonal, and implacably inhuman. For Freud, there is that at the core of the self which has no solicitude for us at all. It is the opposite of Thomas Aquinas's view, for whom there is also an utterly strange power which makes us what we are, but which has more care for us than we have for ourselves.

It is not that the alcoholic wants to drink any more than he wants to bleed to death. It is not a question of wanting. There is nothing in the least subjective about it. Like words, one drink leads to another, and that to another. Just as there is no final word, so there is no final drink. The idea that this crazed drive could be gratified by something determinate—six drinks, say, or even six hundred—is absurd. The alcoholic is in the grip of a Faustian desire, which aims to swallow the whole world and will stop at nothing in order to do so. It is not that he has too little will, but that he has a terrifying, infinite amount of it. He is not a reveler who wallows in the carnal pursuits of wine, women, and song. On the contrary, his drinking is a grim-lipped refusal of the flesh. It is as anti-worldly as the monastic life. It is about as far from a Bacchanalian orgy as the Queen's Christmas message. There is, to be sure, always a chance of redemption—of opting for life over death; but even in the rare event of such a decision, there remains the permanent possibility of consigning oneself to hell once more.

The death drive represents a kind of eternity within time, or a form of death in life. Like evil, it will not submit to spatial or temporal limit. In Hegel's term, it represents a kind of "bad" infinity. We can contrast this with the "good" infinity of what Saint Paul calls grace, or charity. Just as there is no end to desire, so there is no end to charity. There is a bad kind of death-in-life which is the vampirelike existence of the living dead. It is the ghastly twilight world of those who, like the alcoholic or Graham Greene's Pinkie, can be stirred into life only by the taste of destruction on their tongue. But there is also a benign kind of death-in-life which is the "death" of yielding oneself as a gift to others. It is this that the damned cannot do. For them, the self is too precious to be given away. As Kierkegaard remarks, "The torment of despair is precisely the inability to die."[13] In one sense, Kierkegaard argues, those in despair really do want to die: "Far from its being any comfort to the despairer that the despair doesn't consume him, on the contrary this comfort is just what torments him; this is the very thing that keeps the pain alive and life in the pain. For what he . . . despairs over is precisely this: that he cannot consume himself, cannot become nothing . . . what he cannot bear is that he cannot be rid of himself."[14] Those in despair are self-thwarting. They want to die in order to escape from their hapless condition, yet they languish in the grip of a drive that perversely keeps them on the go. If they cannot die, it is because, like Pincher Martin, they are more fearful of nothingness—of the total abandonment of the self—than of their own acute distress. As Friedrich Nietzsche writes, man would rather will anything than not will at all. This, then, is for Kierkegaard the one sickness that cannot be cured by death—for the sickness itself consists precisely in being unable to die.

The alcoholic, then, is in despair. He is trapped in an eternal circuit of hankering and self-loathing from which there seems to be no exit. Metaphorically speaking, he lives in a kind of hell. One of world literature's great drunks, Geoffrey Firmin of Malcolm Lowry's novel *Under the Volcano,* has just this terrible insight: "Suddenly he felt something he never felt before with such shocking certainty. It was that he was in hell himself." But it is not an infernal region that the alcoholic has the least interest in abandoning. For his anguish, as we have seen, is the only thing that keeps him alive. Without this, he fears, he would be dead indeed. The barrier to freedom and happiness, then, is himself. The addict is someone who has become an insuperable obstacle to his own well-being. And this is one way in which he resembles those who are evil. Stuck fast in the grip of the death drive, the damned delight in their own torments, as well as in the suffering of those they prey on, since clinging to their agony is the only alternative to annihilation. They are the panic-stricken and white-knuckled who cannot see how simple it would be to let go. They are ready to will the hellish and monstrous, the disgusting and excremental, as long as this is the price of feeling alive. If they spit in the face of salvation, it is because it would rob them of the frightful gratification which is all that remains to them of human life.

Two quotations may illustrate the point. The first, once again, is from Kierkegaard, who recognises that those in despair are arrogant as well as self-consuming:

> [Despair] wants to be itself in its hatred towards existence, to be itself according to its misery; it does not even defiantly want to be itself, but to be itself in sheer spite; it does not even want to sever itself defiantly from the power which established it; it wants in sheer spite to press itself on that power, importune it, hang on to it out of malice . . . Rebelling against all existence, it thinks it has acquired evidence against existence, against its goodness. The despairer thinks that he himself is this evidence. And it is this that he wants to be; this is the reason he wants to be himself, to be himself in his agony, so as to protest with this agony against all existence. As the weak despairer will hear nothing about what comfort eternity has in store for him, so too with this despairer, but for a different reason: the comfort would be his undoing.[15]

The damned refuse to be saved, since this would deprive them of their adolescent rebellion against the whole of reality.

Evil is a kind of cosmic sulking. It rages most violently against those who threaten to snatch its unbearable wretchedness away from it. Only by persisting in its fury and proclaiming it theatrically to the world can evil provide damning evidence of the bankruptcy of existence. It is living testimony to the folly of creation. If it wants to remain itself for ever and ever, rebuffing death as an insufferable insult to its pride, it is not only because it regards itself as too precious to die. It is also because for it to vanish from the scene would be to let the cosmos off the hook. People might then mistake it for a benign sort of place, gullibly swallowing the sentimental propaganda of its Maker. Yet part of the rage of the damned, as we have seen, is the knowledge that they are parasitic on goodness, as the rebel is dependent on the authority he spurns. They are obsessed with the virtue they despise, and are thus the reverse of religious types who can think of nothing but sex. As Kierkegaard writes, they want to "hang on to [that power] out of malice," vex and harass it constantly, like some stubborn old codger who refuses to die because he enjoys being a constant irritant to his long-suffering wife.

The second quotation comes from Father Zosima, the saintly monk of Dostoevsky's *The Brothers Karamazov*. The Satanic, he declares, "demand that there be no God of life, that God destroy himself and all his creation. And they shall burn everlastingly in the flames of their own hatred, and long for death and for non-being. But death shall not be granted them." If hell is said to be without end, it is because its fires feed on themselves, rather as malice and rancour do. Hellfire cannot be extinguished, any more than a fury that insists on refueling itself. A frenzy which is aimed not just against this or that, but against the very fact of existence, is bound to be without limit. The evil want God and his world to commit suicide, so that they themselves can reign sovereign in the void left behind. But as long as they yearn for non-being, there can be no such vacuum. For that yearning is itself a sign of being. This is another aspect of evil's self-thwarting nature. The very desire for nonexistence keeps the nihilist in existence. Rebellion against creation is part of creation. This is why, as Father Zosima remarks, the damned long to die but are unable to do so. What they lack is the inner depth that might allow them to die for real. Because they are mere parodies of human beings, they lack the resources to relinquish themselves in the hope that they might be reborn. They are proud of being dispossessed of the world; but to rid themselves of their identities would be to lose the self that does the dispossessing.

There are, in any case, good and bad ways of refusing the world. If there is the path of the nihilist, there is also the action of the revolutionary. These are not always easy to tell apart. Rupert Birkin, the hero of D. H. Lawrence's novel *Women in Love,* wants to renounce the present in order to clear the space for a transformed future; but it is hard not to suspect that he is exasperated by material reality as such, not just by the particular historical version of it he confronts. In this sense, he is both the ally and the antagonist of the spiritually vacuous Gerald Crich, a character who is leashed together only by his dominative will and who would fall apart if its force were to slacken.

Alcoholics, of course, are not evil. Dipsomania is a long way from the diabolical. Evil appears on the scene only when those in what one might call ontological pain deflect it onto others as a way of taking flight from themselves. It is as though they seek to break open the bodies of others in order to expose the nullity which lurks inside them. In doing so, they can find in this nothingness a consoling reflection of themselves. At the same time, they can demonstrate that matter is not indestructible. Lumps of the stuff known as human bodies can be squeezed out of existence at one's own hands. The wonder is that people who are dead are purely, totally, and absolutely dead. There are no two ways about it. So at least one kind of absolute survives in an alarmingly provisional world. Killing other people, as Raskolnikov is perhaps out to prove in Dostoevsky's *Crime and Punishment,* shows that absolute acts are possible even in a world of moral relativism, fast food joints, and reality TV. Evil, like religious fundamentalism, is among other things a nostalgia for an older, simpler civilisation, in which there were certitudes like salvation and damnation, and you knew where you stood. Greene's Pinkie is a straitlaced, old-fashioned moralist in just this sense. In a curious sense, evil is a protest against the debased quality of modern existence. The devil is a high-class reactionary who finds modern existence distasteful. It is not even deep enough to be damned. His aim is to inject something a little more spiritually exotic into it.

By setting its face against the spirit of utility, evil also has a seductive smack of radicalism about it, since utility lies at the root of our kind of civilisation. Unlike chartered accountants and real estate agents, evil does not believe that practical results are all that counts. It seeks to reintroduce the idea of God to a sceptical, rationalistic culture, since to kill is to exercise a divine power over others. Murder is our most potent way of robbing God of his monopoly over human life.

Yet the idea that evil is glamourous is one of the great moral mistakes of the modern age. (When I told my young son that I was writing a book on evil he replied, "Wicked!") I have written elsewhere on how this mistake may have arisen.[16] Once the middle classes get their hands on virtue, even vice begins to look appealing. Once the puritan propagandists and evangelical mill owners redefine virtue as thrift, prudence, chastity, abstinence, sobriety, meekness, frugality, obedience, and self-discipline, it is not hard to see why evil should begin to look like a sexier option. As with the magnificent music of Adrian Leverkühn, the devil seems to have all the best tunes. Suburban virtue is a poor thing compared to Satanic vice. We would all rather have a drink with Dickens's Fagin or Emily Brontë's Heathcliff than a chat with the God of John Milton's *Paradise Lost,* who speaks like a constipated civil servant. Everyone loves a rogue.

But do they really? It might be more accurate to say that

everyone loves a lovable rogue. We admire people who thumb their nose at authority, but not rapists or corporate fraudsters. We have a sneaking affection for people who steal salt cellars from the Savoy Hotel, but not for Islamic fundamentalists who rip people limb from limb. It is true that most readers enjoy *Paradise Lost*'s Satan, in all his glowering, doomed defiance of the Almighty. But we enjoy him largely for his more positive qualities (courage, resilience, resoluteness, and so on) rather than for anything specifically evil about him. In fact, there is very little specifically evil about him. Feeding Adam and Eve an apple is not in our eyes the most fearful of transgressions.

By the time middle-class civilisation arrives at its post-modern phase, however, transgression has become all the rage. In postmodern circles, the word itself is almost always used affirmatively, even though it includes strangling babies and plunging hatchets into other people's skulls. Truly to transgress, however, you must believe that the conventions you are bucking have some force. So once transgression itself has become the norm, it ceases to be subversive. Perhaps this is what the psychoanalyst Jacques Lacan had in mind when he observed in his cryptic fashion that if God is dead, nothing is permitted. For permission implies an authority that can grant you a licence; and if such an authority no longer functions, the idea of permission is bound to lose its force. Who in the age of "permissiveness" is doing the permitting? Granting permission implies the possible withholding of it; and in some contemporary circles the very idea of this would be unthinkable.

The jaded sensibility of postmodern culture can no longer find much shock value in sexuality. So it turns instead to evil, or at least to what it guilelessly imagines to be evil: vampires, mummies, zombies, rotting corpses, maniacal laughter, demoniac children, bleeding wallpaper, multicoloured vomit, and so on. None of this of course is evil at all, just plain nasty. As such, it is open to the charge that the novelist Henry James, however questionably, leveled against the poetry of Charles Baudelaire: "Evil for him begins outside and not inside, and consists primarily of a great deal of lurid landscape and unclean furniture . . . Evil is represented as an affair of blood and carrion and physical sickness . . . there must be stinking corpses and starving prostitutes and empty laudanum bottles in order that the poet shall be effectively inspired."[17] Evil here is just a banal theatrics. In James's own writing, by contrast, a whiff of corruption can be detected in, say, the fact that a gentleman discovered alone in a room with a lady who is not his wife is sitting while she is standing.

"Angelic" societies are those whose politics are little more than a set of managerial techniques designed to keep its citizens happy. As such, they are likely to breed the demonic as a backlash to their own blandness. Not only the demonic, in fact, but all kinds of phony alternatives to themselves, from celebrity cults and religious fundamentalism to Satanism and New Age claptrap. Societies that deprive people of some adequate sense-making tend to farm out the manufacture of such meaning to cottage industries like astrology and Kabbalah.

Myriad forms of takeaway transcendence can be snapped up on the cheap. The more tediously angelic our official regimes grow, the more they give birth to a mindless nihilism. A glut of meaning leads to a depletion of it. And the more futile and anarchic social existence grows, the more angelic ideologies, full of pious, hand-on-heart talk of God and national greatness, are needed to contain the dissent and disruption to which this might lead.

Traditionally, evil is seen not as sexy but as mind-numbingly monotonous. Kierkegaard speaks of the demonic in *The Concept of Anxiety* as "the contentless, the boring." Like some modernist art, it is all form and no substance. Hannah Arendt, writing of the petit-bourgeois banality of Adolf Eichmann, sees him as having neither depth nor any demonic dimension. But what if this depthlessness is exactly what the demonic is like? What if it is more like a minor official than a flamboyant tyrant? Evil is boring because it is lifeless. Its seductive allure is purely superficial. There may be a hectic flush on its visage, but, as with the characters of Mann's *The Magic Mountain,* it is the deceptive glow of the diseased. It is fever rather than vitality. Like the slimy Mr. Hyde in Robert Louis Stevenson's story, the horror is that something which is actually inorganic can seem so deceptively energetic. Evil is a transitional state of being—a domain wedged between life and death, which is why we associate it with ghosts, mummies, and vampires. Anything which is neither quite dead nor quite alive can become an image of it. It is boring because it keeps doing the same dreary thing, trapped as it is between life and death. The narrator of *The Third Policeman* will keep returning to the police station for all eternity, in a kind of infernal recurrence. But evil is also boring because it is without real substance. It has, for example, no notion of emotional intricacies. Like a Nazi rally, it appears spectacular but is secretly hollow. It is as much a parody of genuine life as the goosestep is a parody of walking.

Evil is philistine, kitsch-ridden, and banal. It has the ludicrous pomposity of a clown seeking to pass himself off as an emperor. It defends itself against the complexities of human experience with a reach-me-down dogma or a cheap slogan. Like Pinkie in *Brighton Rock,* it is dangerous precisely because of its lethal innocence. It has no grasp of the human world and is as bemused by a genuine outbreak of emotion as the British royal family. It has no savoir faire, and is as much at a loss as a toddler when confronted with grief or euphoria or sexual passion. If it believes in absolutely nothing, it is because it does not have enough interior life to be capable of doing so. Hell is not a scene of unspeakable obscenities. If it were, it might well be worth applying to join. Hell is being talked at for all eternity by a man in an anorak who has mastered every detail of the sewage system of South Dakota.

For Thomas Aquinas, the more a thing succeeds in realising its true nature, the more it can be said to be good. The perfection of a thing, he argues, depends on the extent to which it has achieved actuality. Things are good if they flourish in the way appropriate to them. The more a thing thrives in its own peculiar way, the finer it is. Every being, considered as such, is good. And if God is the most perfect being of all, it is because he is pure self-realisation. Unlike us, there is nothing that he could be that he isn't. So for Aquinas there is no such thing as a being which is bad. Having Billy Connolly or the Peruvians around the place is a good thing in itself, even if they are all capable from time to time of actions which are less than admirable. The poet William Blake sometimes pretends to take the side of the devil, not least in his *Proverbs of Heaven and Hell.* He seizes the conventional opposition between good and evil and mischievously inverts it, making evil the positive category and good the negative one. But this is simply a tactic for scandalising respectable middle-class Christians, with their anemic notion of virtue. Blake's true belief is summarised in a single phrase: "Everything that lives is holy."

Thomas Aquinas thoroughly agreed. Like his great predecessor Saint Augustine, but also like some ancient Greek and Judaic thought, Aquinas regards evil not as something existent, but as a kind of deficiency of being. Evil for him is lack, negation, defectiveness, deprivation. It is a kind of malfunctioning, a flaw at the heart of being. Physical pain, for example, is evil because it is a snarl-up in the way the body works. It is an incapacity for an abundance of life. For his part, Augustine takes this line largely because he wants to argue against the Manicheans, who held the Gnostic theory that matter is evil in itself. For them, evil is a positive force or substance which invades us from the outside. It is the science-fiction view of reality. On the contrary, Augustine argues, evil is no kind of thing or force at all. To think so is to make a fetish of it, as in the horror movies. It springs from us, not from some alien power beyond us; and it springs from us because it is the effect of human freedom. It is, he comments, "the inclination of what has more being for what has less being."

As such, evil is a kind of spiritual slumming. The doctrine of original sin, which Augustine did more to frame than any other early Christian thinker, is among other things a protest against a reified or superstitious view of evil. Evil is an ethical affair, not a question of certain toxic entities which infect our flesh. It is a pity that Augustine then had to blot his copybook by going on to claim that original sin was transmitted by the act of sexual reproduction. That, predictably, is the only piece of his argument that has lingered in the historical memory. Such a view is perhaps taking materialism a little too far. In fact, some of the more absurd excesses of the Catholic church spring not from a falsely spiritualist view of the world, but from a crudely materialist approach to actions and bodies.

If evil is nothing in itself, then not even an all-powerful God could have created it. Contrary to the popular prejudice that the Almighty can do whatever takes his fancy, there are actually all sorts of activities that are beyond his reach. He cannot join the Girl Guides, comb his hair, tie his shoelaces, or pare his fingernails. He cannot create a square triangle. He cannot literally be the father of Jesus Christ, since he does not have testicles. And he cannot create nothingness, since noth-ingness is not something you can either create or destroy. Only a trick of grammar makes us think otherwise. Even the Almighty must be bound by the laws of logic. The fact that evil is nothing positive does not of course mean that it has no positive effects. It is not like pretending that pain is an illu-sion. Darkness and hunger are nothing positive either, but nobody would deny that they have real effects. (It is true, as we have seen, that Flann O'Brien's de Selby regards darkness as a positive entity, but in this he belongs to an aberrant minority.) A hole is not something you can put in your pocket, but a hole in the head is real enough.

There are those who feel uneasy about this way of view-ing evil. How can one possibly speak of Mao's monstrous purges, or those who perished in the Nazi concentration camps, as victims of a simple deficiency? Doesn't this risk underestimating the terrifying positivity of evil?[18] It is here, I think, that psychoanalytic theory can ride to the rescue, allow-ing us to maintain that evil is a kind of deprivation while still acknowledging its formidable power. The power in question, as we have seen already, is essentially that of the death drive, turned outward so as to wreak its insatiable spitefulness on a fellow human being. Yet this furious violence involves a kind of lack—an unbearable sense of non-being, which must, so to speak, be taken out on the other. It is also oriented to another kind of absence: the nullity of death itself. Here, then, terrify-ing force and utter vacuousness come together. In his *Church*

Dogmatics the theologian Karl Barth points out that evil is a nothingness of corruption and destruction, not just of absence and deprivation.

The evil, then, are those who are deficient in the art of living. For Aristotle, living is something you have to get good at through constant practice, like playing the saxophone. It is something that the wicked have never quite got the hang of. Neither, for that matter, have any of us. It is just that most of us are better at it than Jack the Ripper. That we are all defective in this respect might come as a surprise to visitors from another world, who might reasonably expect to stumble upon a handful of perfect examples of the human species, along with a number of botched versions. It would seem as reasonable as expecting that there are a number of excellent apples around as well as a lot of rotten ones. The fact that all human beings without exception are dysfunctional in one way or another might seem to visiting aliens as bizarre as the idea that all the paintings in New York's Guggenheim Museum are fakes. If the evil are grossly deficient in the art of living, the rest of us are moderately so.

In this sense, though evil is not the kind of thing we bump into every day, it has an intimate relation to ordinary life. The death drive is nothing in the least special, and there is no shortage of sadists. Or think of that malicious delight in other people's misfortunes that the Germans call *Schadenfreude*. The philosopher David Hume claims in his *Treatise of Human Nature* that we derive pleasure from the pleasure of others, but also some pain; and that though we feel pained by another's pain, it also yields us some pleasure. This in Hume's view is merely a fact of life, not some diabolical perversity. There is no particular reason to feel scandalised by it.

Colin McGinn regards the common-or-garden feeling of envy as perhaps the closest most of us come to evil, at least in the sense in which we have been defining the word.[19] The envious are pained by another's pleasure, since it throws into relief their own unfulfilled existences. As Milton's Satan laments:

> . . . the more I see
> Pleasures about me, so much more I feel
> Torment within me, as from the hateful siege
> Of contraries; all good to me becomes
> Bane, and in heav'n much worse would be my
> > state . . .
> Nor hope to be myself less miserable
> By what I seek, but others to make such
> As I, though thereby worse to me redound.
> For only in destroying I find ease
> To my relentless thoughts.

Rather as Freud thought that everyday life had its psychopathological features, so we can find analogues of evil in the everyday world. Like a good many rare phenomena, evil has its roots in the commonplace. Adolf Eichmann, who looked more like a harassed bank clerk than an architect of genocide, is one illustration of this fact. To this extent, evil is not just an elitist affair, as some of its practitioners would prefer to imagine. But neither should this lead us to overestimate how pervasive it is. Plain wickedness, like destroying whole communities for financial gain or being prepared to use nuclear weapons, is a great deal more common than pure evil. Evil is not something we should lose too much sleep over.

CHAPTER THREE

Job's Comforters

Whenever some tragedy or natural disaster takes place these days, one can be sure to find a group of men and women holding homemade placards inscribed with the pregnant word "Why?" These people are not looking for factual explanations. They know very well that the earthquake was the result of a fissure deep in the earth, or that the murder was the work of a serial killer released too soon from custody. "Why?" does not mean, "What was the cause of this?" It is more of a lament than a query. It is a protest against some profound lack of logic in the world. It is a reaction to what seems the brute senselessness of things.

One branch of traditional thought, known as theodicy, has tried to account for this apparent senselessness. The word "theodicy" literally means "justifying God." So the point of trying to account for why the world seems so lamentably askew is to defend a supposedly all-loving God against the charge of having catastrophically failed in his duties. Theodicy tries to explain the existence of evil in ways that would let the Almighty off the hook. The greatest artistic project of this kind in British literary culture is John Milton's mighty epic *Paradise Lost,* in which the poet seeks to "justify the ways of God to men" by accounting for why humanity is in such a wretched state. For Milton the revolutionary, this includes the question of why the political paradise he had hoped to see ushered in by the English civil war had gone so miserably awry. For some readers, however, the poet's pious attempts to exonerate the Almighty simply result in damning him even deeper. Trying to justify God by providing him with elaborate arguments in his own defence, as the poem does, is bound to bring him down to our own level. Gods are not supposed to argue, any more than princes or judges are.

The theologian Kenneth Surin points out that the more one views the world as a rational, harmonious whole, in the manner of the eighteenth-century European Enlightenment, the more pressing the problem of evil becomes.[1] Modern attempts to explain evil really stem from the cosmic optimism of the Enlightenment. Evil is the dark shadow that the light of

Reason cannot banish. It is the joker in the cosmic pack, the grit in the oyster, the out-of-place factor in a tidy world. To explain this anomaly, theodicy has a number of arguments on offer. There is, to begin with, what one might call the Boy Scout, or cold-shower, case, which sees the existence of evil as essential for the building of moral character. It is the kind of argument that one imagines would appeal to Prince Andrew, who remarked while fighting in the Falklands war that being shot at was excellent for character-building. On this view, evil provides us with a chance to do good and exercise responsibility. A world without evil would be too bland to provoke us into virtuous action. The devil in Dostoevsky's *The Brothers Karamazov* adopts just such an argument to justify his own existence: his role, he informs Ivan Karamazov, is to act as a kind of friction or negativity in God's creation, a cross-grained element that prevents it from collapsing of sheer boredom. He is, he remarks, the "x in an indeterminate equation"—the "requisite negativity" in the universe without which pure harmony and absolute order would break out and put an end to everything.

In the end, the case for evil as a necessary disruption or resistance comes down to the claim that having your entrails extracted, burned, and then stuffed into your mouth makes a man of you. Like being a Marine, it offers you a rare chance to show what stuff you are made of. God, writes Richard Swinburne, is justified in allowing "Hiroshima, Belsen, the Lisbon

Earthquake or the Black Death," so that human beings can live in a real world rather than a toy one.[2] It is hard to believe that anyone but an Oxbridge don could pen such a sentiment.

It is true that good can sometimes come from evil. There are those arrogant types for whom, one suspects, the odd spot of severe misfortune might not come amiss. Some have argued that the apparent collapse of meaning in the modern world may look alarming, but it is really a blessing in disguise. Once we have realised that things are not meaningful in themselves, we are free to assign them whatever significances we find most fruitful. Out of the rubble of traditional meanings we can create our own more serviceable ones. So we can glean profit in the end from what looks like catastrophe.

Yet good does not always spring from evil; and even when it does, this is scarcely enough to justify it. Arrogant types might find some less drastic way to learn a little humility than losing their limbs. No doubt some good came out of the Holocaust, not least the courage and comradeship of some of its victims; but to imagine that any amount of human kindness could have justified it would be a moral obscenity. Though Jesus is portrayed by the New Testament as spending much of his time curing the sick, he never once advises the ill and infirm to reconcile themselves to their suffering. On the contrary, he seems to regard their afflictions as the work of the devil. He does not suggest that heaven will be adequate compensation for their woes. Even if suffering makes you gentler and wiser, it is still bad for you. It is still a bad thing that *this* was the way you managed to become gentler and wiser, rather than some other way.

This takes us back to the theme of the fortunate Fall. Does "fortunate" mean that it was a good thing that it happened? Was our break with Nature and our entry upon history a positive event? Not necessarily. History brings with it some magnificent achievements, to be sure—but only at the price of a colossal amount of wretchedness. Marxists are those who believe that these two aspects of the human narrative are closely interconnected. Perhaps we would all have been better off as amoebae. If the human species ends up destroying itself, which seems a plausible end to its astonishingly barbarous history, there might be many who pass their last moments thinking just this. Was evolution, and the human history to which it eventually gave birth, one long, ghastly error? Shouldn't the whole thing have been called off before it got so egregiously out of hand? Certainly there have been thinkers who have believed so. Arthur Schopenhauer, as we have seen, was one of them.

In *Paradise Lost,* John Milton is rather more ambiguous on the question. As a revolutionary Puritan who believes in the necessity of conflict, Milton is not greatly enthused by the harmonious yet static world of Eden. Yet as a utopian thinker who yearns for the kingdom of God, and who dared to hope that the Puritan party in the English Civil War might help to bring it about on earth, there is a side of Milton which is homesick for the happy garden. Perhaps the truth in Milton's eyes is that it would have been better had we never been expelled from our first home—but that given that we were, we now have a chance to attain an even more resplendent bliss.

The point, surprisingly enough, is relevant not only to Milton but to Marxism. Are Marxists committed to believing that the evils of capitalism are also a good thing, because they will lead eventually to a more desirable condition known as socialism? Certainly Marx himself is loud in his praise of capitalism as the most revolutionary mode of production history has ever witnessed. It is, to be sure, an exploitative system that has visited untold horrors on humanity. Yet in Marx's view it also fosters the powers of men and women to a hitherto unknown degree. Its rich traditions of liberalism and Enlightenment represent vital legacies for any viable socialism. So is history's "Fall" into capitalism not only fortunate but necessary? Could there be any true socialism without it? Isn't capitalism necessary to develop the wealth of society to the point where socialism can take it over and reorganise it in the interests of everyone?

Some Marxists, to be sure, have argued just such a case. The Mensheviks of revolutionary Russia are among the most familiar examples. If this case is true, then Marxism is an example of a theodicy. It involves trying to justify historical evils by insisting on the good which will ultimately spring from them. In the view of some Marxists, the slavery of the ancient world, however morally regrettable, was necessary because it led to the more "progressive" regime of feudalism. Something similar might perhaps be argued about the shift from feudalism to capitalism. Not many who call themselves Marxists these days, however, would defend such a bold-faced proposition. For one thing, they would point out, capitalism does not follow with iron necessity from feudalism. Nor does socialism inevitably follow from capitalism, as a quick glance around the globe might confirm. Given that capitalism did in fact emerge, socialists can indeed strive to place its accumulated spiritual and material resources at the service of humanity as a whole. All the same, it would have been preferable if there had been some other way of achieving this goal, rather as for Milton it would probably have been better had the Fall from Eden never happened in the first place. Socialists could even argue (though hardly any of them do) that it might have been preferable had human history itself never come about. Even if we are able to construct a just society, it may not prove much recompense for the atrocious nature of the past and present. It cannot redeem the dead. It does not make slavery, Bob Hope, or the Thirty Years War retrospectively tolerable. History, it is true, may well have unfolded differently. But given that it has happened as it has, it is not unreasonable to claim that, socialism or no socialism, it would have been better if it had never come about at all. The claim may not be true. But it is not unreasonable.

Even if good can come from evil, inquires the philosopher Brian Davies, "what are we to make of someone [i.e., God] who *organises* evils so that goods might arise from them?"[3] Couldn't he have found some more agreeable way of testing our mettle than dengue fever, Britney Spears, or tarantulas? Perhaps evil is inevitable in this particular kind of world; but then why couldn't God have created a different one? Some theologians contend that God could not have created a *material* world which did not involve pain and suffering. On this theory, if we want sensual pleasures, or if we just want bodies, we have to put up with the odd spot of agony. The philosopher Leibniz claimed that what we have is the best of all possible worlds; but for some other thinkers, the idea of the best of all possible worlds is as incoherent as the idea of the greatest prime number. Given any particular world, you can always imagine a better one (one with Kate Winslet living next door to you, for example).

Then there is what one might call the Big Picture argument, which claims that evil is not really evil, just good which we fail to recognise as such. If we were able to see the whole cosmic picture, look at the world from a God's-eye viewpoint, we would recognise that what appears to us to be evil plays an essential part in some beneficent whole. Without this apparent evil, that whole would not function as it should. Once we put things in context, what looks bad is seen to be good. A small child may be horrified at the sight of a woman sawing off a human finger, failing to grasp that the woman in question is a surgeon and the finger in question is damaged beyond repair. Evil on this account is not seeing the wood for the trees. It appears to us, myopic creatures that we are, that roasting small infants over fires is rather less than desirable;

but if only we could widen our angle of understanding, grasping the part this action plays in some greater plan, we would see its point, and might even enthusiastically lend a hand. There have been more convincing arguments in the history of human thought. A back-to-front version of this case crops up in Friedrich Nietzsche, who claims that if you assent to a single joyful experience, you also assent to all the sorrow and evil in the world, since all things are interwoven.

Some see evil as a mystery. Yet in one sense the reason why the human world is less than perfect is blatantly obvious. It is because human beings are free to maim, exploit, and oppress one another. This does not account for what some call natural evil (earthquakes, disease, and the like), though men and women today have more reason than their forebears to be aware just how many so-called natural evils are in fact the work of our own hands. The modern age progressively blurs the line between Nature and history. The apocalyptic tradition sees the world as ending in fire and flood, tumbling mountains, shattered skies, heavenly convulsions, cosmic portents of various kinds. It is just that it never occurred to these visionaries that we ourselves, puny animals that we are, might turn out to be responsible for this grand scenario. Apocalypse was always something visited upon us rather than generated by us. But we are perfectly capable of doing it all by ourselves.

The question for religious believers is not really why there is wickedness in the world. The answer to that is pretty obvious. There is no mystery about why a pimp should lock up thirty imported Albanian sex slaves in a British brothel. The question for believers is why human beings were created free to do such things in the first place. Some believers hold that for humans not to be created free would be a contradiction in terms. This is because the Creator in question is God, who himself is pure freedom. To be made in God's image and likeness is precisely not to be a puppet. If those he creates are to be authentically his, they must live according to his own free life; and if they are free, then they must be free to go awry. On this theory, any animal capable of doing good must logically be capable of doing evil as well.

But does this really follow? It is not at all obvious that God was incapable of creating men and women who were free, but not free to go wrong. That, after all, is how he himself is supposed to be. God cannot traffic in Albanian sex slaves, not only because he has no wallet in which to keep his ill-gotten gains but because to do so would run contrary to the sort of being he is. And unlike us, God cannot be at odds with himself. We saw earlier that for mainstream Christian theology things are good in themselves, and evil is a kind of bungling or privation of being. The more things flourish, doing what they are supposed to do, the better they are. It follows that a tiger who chews off your arm is good, because it is doing the kind of thing tigers are supposed to get up to. The only problem is that its way of flourishing is at loggerheads with your own. Viruses, too, do their own innocent, viruslike thing. There is nothing in the least objectionable about viruses in themselves. No doubt some dissident group or other will get round sooner or later to protesting that viruses have rights, waving indignant messages on placards outside hospitals and assaulting physicians who try to eradicate them. The problem is simply that in behaving in their own uniquely creative manner, viruses tend to kill off human beings, who are consequently unable to behave in *their* own uniquely creative manner. Why could not God have created a universe in which the flourishing of one kind of thing was not in conflict with that of another? Why does the world seem such a free-market sort of place?

Some theologians today, confronted with the problem of evil, more or less take God's line in the Book of Job. To ask after God's reasons for allowing evil, so they claim, is to imagine him as some kind of rational or moral being, which is the last thing he is. To think so is rather like picturing aliens as green-coloured, sulphur-breathing humanoids with triangular eyes but (sinisterly enough) no kidneys. All this testifies to is the paucity of the human imagination. Even the utterly strange turns out to be a thinly disguised version of ourselves. God is not to be seen as a supersized version of a moral agent, with duties, responsibilities, obligations, opportunities for good behaviour, and the like. This, so it is argued, is an Enlightenment view of the Almighty, one which tries to cut him down to size by modeling him idolatrously on ourselves. As the philosopher Mary Midgley observes, "If God is there, he is surely something bigger and more mysterious than a corrupt or stupid official."[4] God does not lie within the scope of human logic, as he is quick to point out to Job in the Old Testament. When Job bewails his adversity, asking why God should have visited these hardships on an innocent like himself, his comforters offer him various posh-sounding pseudo-explanations. Perhaps, for example, his ancestors committed certain sins for which he is being punished. Finally God himself steps in and brushes these spineless suggestions contemptuously aside. Far from offering Job an account of why he has allowed him to suffer, he more or less tells him to go to hell. What can you possibly know about me? is the brunt of his testy intervention. How dare you imagine that you can apply your moral and rational codes to me? Isn't this like a snail trying to second-guess a scientist? Who the hell do you think you are? In the end, Job decides to love God "for naught"—to love him without regard for merits or demerits, reward or retribution, with a love as gratuitous as the scourges he has endured.

"After Auschwitz," writes Richard J. Bernstein, "it is obscene to continue to speak of evil and suffering as something to be justified by, or reconciled with, a benevolent cosmological scheme."[5] But wasn't it always? Why only after Auschwitz? Plenty of people found such explanations offensive long before the Nazi concentration camps. We have no answer, then, to why God "allows" six million Jews to be murdered, if "allows" is the right word. Religious believers might as well give up searching for such explanations as a bad job. All of the arguments produced so far are bogus, and one or two of them are morally outrageous. This is why Kant wrote an essay entitled "On the Miscarriage of All Philosophical Attempts at a Theodicy." Theodicy, writes the philosopher Paul Ricoeur, is a "mad project."[6] If this is the best Christians can do, they had better admit defeat and become—at least on this momentous issue—agnostics. Even so, they will still need to reckon with the fact that the existence of evil is an extremely powerful argument against the existence of God.

"A great deal of evil," writes Midgley, "is caused by quiet, respectable, unaggressive motives like sloth, fear, avarice and greed."[7] In the terms of this book, these motives would count more as wicked or immoral than as evil; but the general point is surely valid. For the most part, it is old-fashioned self-interest and rapacity we have to fear, not evil. Monstrous acts are by no means always committed by monstrous individuals. CIA torturers no doubt make devoted husbands and fathers. No single individual is usually responsible for military carnage, despite loose talk of Caesar defeating whole tribes. Those who steal pension funds or pollute whole regions of the planet are quite often mild-mannered individuals who believe that business is business. And that this is so should be seen as a source of hope. The point is that most wickedness is institutional. It is the result of vested interests and anonymous processes, not of the malign acts of individuals. One should not, to be sure, underestimate the importance of such acts, just as one should not be so excessively sophisticated as to reject the idea of conspiracies. It is a fact that men and women with shady intentions gather from time to time in what these days are smoke-free rooms to plot some moral outrage or other. For the most part, however, such outrages are the product of particular systems.

Because most forms of wickedness are built into our social systems, the individuals who serve those systems may well be unaware of the gravity of their actions. This is not to say that they are mere puppets of historical forces. It is generally the case, as Noam Chomsky once remarked, that intellectuals do not need to speak truth to power because power knows the truth anyway. Even if it does, however, many individuals who act in politically obnoxious ways are sensitive, conscientious men and women who believe they are selflessly serving the state, the company, God, or the future of the Free World, terms which for some right-wing Americans are pretty well synonymous. Such people may regard their own disreputable actions as distasteful but essential, like a John Le Carré secret agent. Extracting other people's fingernails is not the way they would choose to act in an ideal world. This is one reason why those who extract other people's fingernails, and above all those who instruct them to do so, can still pay lip service to moral values without feeling too much of a sense of incongruity. Those values may be real to them; it is just that they occupy a different sphere from business or Realpolitik. And these spheres are not especially expected to intersect. As the cynic remarked, it is when religion starts interfering with your everyday life that it is time to give it up.

False consciousness, then, is something we have reason to feel thankful for. If many of those who engage in disreputable acts were not in its grip, at least to some degree, we would be forced to conclude that a great many men and women are dyed-in-the-wool villains. And this might then raise the question of whether they either deserved or were capable of building a social order superior to what we have at present. Marx and Engels did not draw on the concept of ideology in order to make a radical politics look feasible, but there is a relation between the two even so. The fact that men and women are so deeply conditioned by their circumstances often presents an obstacle to political change; but it also suggests that they need not be written off as beyond political redemption. Ironically, what the humanists may really have going for them is false consciousness. If people who maim and exploit really do not know what they are doing, to borrow a celebrated line from the New Testament, then they are no doubt morally mediocre rather than utter scoundrels. Even if they only partly grasp the significance of what they are up to, or know exactly what they are doing but regard it as indispensable for some honourable end, they are perhaps not beyond the pale. I say "perhaps" because Stalin and Mao murdered for what they saw as an honourable end, and if they are not beyond the moral pale then it is hard to know who is.

If it were not true that acts of wickedness are very often the result of false conceptions, overbearing interests, and historical forces, the implications might be dire indeed. We might be forced to conclude that the human species is simply not worth preserving. Schopenhauer considered that anyone who thought it was must be deeply deluded. To him, human life seemed simply not worth the effort. All it consisted of, he believed, was "momentary gratification, fleeting pleasure conditioned by wants, much and long suffering, constant struggle, *bellum omnium,* everything a hunter and everything hunted, want, need and anxiety, shrieking and howling; and this goes on *in saecula saeculorum* or until once again the crust of the planet breaks."[8]

One might object that this portrait of human existence is a trifle selective. Some rather central features seem to have been unaccountably omitted. But even if one grants that Schopenhauer leaves out just about everything that makes life worth living, there is still a problem. Of course there is love as well as war, laughter as well as howling, joy as well as torture. But have these two sets of features, positive and negative, really balanced out in the account book of human history to date? The answer is surely no. On the contrary, the negative aspects have not only been predominant, but in many times and places overwhelmingly so. Hegel regarded history as "the slaughter bench on which the happiness of peoples, the wisdom of states, and the virtue of individuals have been sacrificed." The epochs of happiness in history, he considered, are blank pages. He also writes of "the evil, the wickedness, and the downfall of the most flourishing empires the human spirit has created," along with "the untold miseries of human beings."[9] And this from a thinker who is regularly accused of an excess of historical optimism! "A philosophy," writes Schopenhauer, "in which one does not hear, between the pages, tears, howling and chattering of teeth, and the frightful din of general, reciprocal murder, is no philosophy."[10] It is a vision shared by Theodor Adorno, who wrote of the "permanent catastrophe" of human history.

Virtue has hardly ever flourished in public affairs other than briefly and precariously. The values we admire—mercy, compassion, justice, loving kindness—have been largely confined to the private domain. Most human cultures have been narratives of rapine, greed, and exploitation. The tumultuous century from which we have just emerged was stained with blood from one end to the other, marked by millions of unnecessary deaths. We have become so accustomed to viewing political life as violent, corrupt, and oppressive that we have ceased to be surprised by the curious persistence of this condition. Would we not expect, simply by the mythical law of averages, to stumble upon a great many more outbreaks of sweetness and light in the annals of human history?

The point can be put another way. It is a barroom cliché that there is good and bad in us all. Human beings are mixed, ambiguous, morally hybrid creatures. But if this is so, why has not the good risen more often to the political surface? It must surely be because of the nature of social and political history—of structures, institutions, and processes of power. The conservative view of the matter is rather different. Humans are not just morally hybrid, in some feeble piece of liberal fence-sitting. On the contrary, they are for the most part corrupt, indolent creatures who require constant discipline and authority if anything of value is to be dredged out of them. From this viewpoint, those who expect too much of human nature—socialists, libertarians, and the like—will find themselves cruelly disenchanted. They will be tempted to idealise men and women to death. For conservatives, by contrast, the margins for human improvement are dispiritingly narrow. They believe in original sin but not in redemption, whereas some rose-tinted liberals believe in redemption but not in original sin. In this Panglossian view, men and women can pull through because there is nothing calamitous enough about our condition to prevent it. For a certain naive libertarianism, there are indeed grave impediments to human well-being, but they are almost all on the outside. The human capacities which these forces block are seen as inherently positive. The only reason we are not free is that something is standing in our way. If this were true, it is surprising that revolution and emancipation do not occur more frequently. The fact that we need to be emancipated from ourselves is doubtless one reason why they do not.

Radicals, by contrast, must maintain a precarious balancing act here. On the one hand, they must be brutally realistic about the depth and tenacity of human corruption to date. Otherwise there can be nothing very insistent about the project of transforming our condition. Those who sentimentally indulge humanity do it no favours. On the contrary, they act as a barrier to change. On the other hand, this corruption cannot be such that transformation is out of the question. Too sanguine a reading of history leads to the belief that no thoroughgoing change is necessary, while too gloomy a view of it suggests that such change is impossible to come by.

How, then, is the radical project not to be disarmed by the sheer recalcitrance of historical injustice to date? How is realism not to undermine hope? It would seem at times that the more pressing the need for political change, the less possible it is. This was the situation in which the Russian Bolsheviks found themselves in 1917, the year of the Soviet revolution. In the face of Tsarist autocracy, a dearth of liberal and civic institutions, an impoverished peasantry, and a sorely exploited proletariat, revolution appeared to the Bolsheviks to be imperative. Yet these were also some of the very factors which made such a change so arduous. As Lenin once remarked, it was the backwardness of Russian society which made the revolution relatively easy to launch. A strike at the Tsarist state, given its monopoly of absolute power, was to prove more or less sufficient. But it was the very same backwardness, Lenin added, which made the revolution so hard to sustain once it had taken place. A hideously disfigured brand of socialism came about in the twentieth century because socialism proved least possible where it was most urgent. And this is certainly one of the major tragedies of that epoch.

What prevents the radical from sliding into political despair is materialism. I mean by this the belief that most violence and injustice are the result of material forces, not of the vicious dispositions of individuals. It belongs to such materialism, for example, not to expect people who are deprived and oppressed to behave like Saint Francis of Assisi. Sometimes they do; but when they do, it is the sheer unexpectedness of it that is most impressive. Virtue depends to some extent on material well-being. You cannot enjoy decent relationships with others when you are starving. The opposite of materialism here is moralism—the belief that good and bad deeds are quite independent of their material contexts, and that this is part of what makes them what they are. Radicals do not believe that to transform those surroundings would be to produce a society of saints. Far from it. There are plenty of reasons, Freudian and otherwise, for believing that a fair amount of human nastiness would survive even the most deep-seated of political changes. It belongs to any authentic materialism to be conscious of the limits of the political, which includes an awareness of how things stand with us as a material species. Even so, the radical claim is that life could be feasibly much improved for a great many people. And this is surely no more than political realism.

Those who are engaged in a material struggle to survive are unlikely to be radiantly virtuous for just that reason, not because they are all closet Pinkies or mini-Leverkühns. It is partly because of the artificial scarcity of resources engendered by class-society, as well as by its denial of human recognition to so many millions, that the historical record has been so barbarous and benighted. Morality cannot be divorced from power. Moreover, just as those who are treated cruelly tend to become denatured, so too are all kinds of exotic vices bred among the rulers themselves. Like some celebrity superstars, many of the rich and powerful come to believe after a while that they are immortal and invincible. They would not concede this if you asked them, of course, but this is the belief to which their behaviour attests. And when it comes to belief, one should look at what people do, not at what they say. As a result of this belief, such individuals come to wield the destructive power of gods. Only those whose circumstances make them conscious of their mortality are likely to feel solidarity with others of their kind.

I have argued that a great deal of immoral behaviour is bound up with material institutions, and that, to this extent, rather like original sin it is not entirely the fault of those who engage in it. In fact, what I have proposed is a materialist understanding of that doctrine. Actions can be iniquitous without those who perform them being so. The same goes for goodness. Scoundrels can occasionally be Good Samaritans. From an historical viewpoint, good actions are arguably more important than good individuals. As long as you help to operate the famine relief system, the fact that you are doing so to impress your boyfriend with your altruism is really neither here nor there. But what about evil? Here the distinction between acts and people would seem much less secure. Can there be evil acts without evil persons to execute them? Not if the argument of this book holds water. For evil is a condition of being as well as a quality of behaviour. Two actions may look the same, but one may be evil and one may not. Think, for example, of the difference between someone who practises sadism for erotic pleasure in a consensual sexual relationship, and someone who forces excruciating pain on another person in order to assuage his own nauseous sense of nonbeing.

If evil requires a human subject, however, what about the Nazis? Whose subjective state of being led to Auschwitz? Hitler's? The whole of the party vanguard? The national psyche? These are not easy questions to answer. Perhaps the best we can venture is that evil in Nazi Germany, as in similar situations, worked at very different levels. There were those on the ground who conspired in an evil project not because they themselves were evil, but because as members of the armed forces or other minor functionaries they felt compelled to do so. There were others who eagerly took part in the project (thugs, patriots, casual anti-Semites and the like) and who were therefore more culpable, but who could hardly be described as evil. There were also those who committed unspeakably atrocious deeds, but not because they reaped any particular gratification from doing so. Eichmann may well fall into this category. And then there were those, presumably like Hitler himself, who indulged in fantasies of annihilation, and who can probably be spoken of as authentically evil. Perhaps one can also speak tentatively of a national psyche—of fantasies which gripped and infected those who did not concoct them themselves, to the point where they, too, were afflicted through Nazi propaganda by a sickening sense of being invaded and undermined by alien slime.

If my argument about morality and material conditions has any force, then an important consequence seems to follow from it. We cannot pass reliable moral judgment on the human species because we have never been able to observe it other than in desperately deformed conditions. We simply cannot say what men and women might have been like if conditions had been otherwise. There are those who believe that the truth about the humanity emerges only when you subject people to extreme pressure. Force their backs to the wall, confront them (for example) in some room full of light with what terrifies them most in the world, and they will reveal themselves for what they are. But this is palpably untrue. Probably most individuals would kill others for food and water under certain conditions. But this says very little about the customary state of their souls.

Men and women under intense pressure are generally incapable of being at their finest. It is true that some people are said to be at their best in a crisis. The British, for example, are supposed to display this virtue. They pass the time between crises patiently waiting for another opportunity for extraordinary heroism to arise. But such people are in a minority. If men and women under pressure need those constraints to be lifted, it is not only for the sake of their health but because only then will they have a chance to find out who they really are, or have the chance to become what they want to become. In Marx's view, everything that has happened to date in history has not really been history at all. Instead, it constitutes what he calls "pre-history." It is just one or another variant on the drearily persistent theme of exploitation. Only by breaking through into history proper will we have a chance to discover what we are morally made of. This, for sure, may not turn out to be all that palatable. Perhaps we shall discover that we were monsters all along. But at least we shall now be in a position to see ourselves straight, without the distorted vision bred by an incessant struggle for resources or the brutal imposition of power.

In a sense, the moral absolutists are right. The distinction that matters is indeed one between good and bad. But not in the sense they imagine. Morally speaking, what really divides people is whether or not they acknowledge that history to date has been for the most part a fable of bloodshed and despotism; that violence has been far more typical of the species than civilised conduct; and that a great many men and women born on the planet would almost certainly have been better off never having seen the light of day. Some leftists will feel uneasy with these dourly Schopenhaurian sentiments. They may strike them as luridly defeatist, and as such in danger of sapping political morale. There are leftists for whom pessimism is a kind of thought crime, just as there are chronically upbeat Americans for whom all negativity is a form of nihilism. But the root of all political wisdom is realism. Thomas Hardy knew that only by taking a cool look at the worst might one grope towards the better.

Today, ironically, a mindless progressivism poses a greater threat to political change than an awareness of the nightmare of history. The true antirealists are those like the scientist Richard Dawkins, with his staggeringly complacent belief that we are all becoming kinder and more civilised. "Most of us in the twenty-first century," he writes in *The God Delusion*, "are . . . way ahead of our counterparts in the Middle Ages, or in the time of Abraham, or even as recently as the 1920s. The whole wave keeps moving, and even the vanguard of an earlier century . . . would find itself way behind the laggers of a later century. There are local and temporary setbacks such as the United States is suffering from its government in the early 2000s. But over the longer timescale, the progressive trend is unmistakeable and will continue."[11]

It is true that Dawkins is speaking here for the most part (though not exclusively) of the growth of liberal values. There has indeed been a gratifying amount of (highly uneven) progress in this area. So Dawkins, despite that loftily dogmatic "and will continue" (does he have a crystal ball?), is quite right to insist on the preciousness of this development, in the teeth of those for whom the very idea of progress is no more than an imperialist myth. It is true that some things get better in some respects. Those who doubt the reality of progress might try having their teeth pulled without anesthetics. They might also try affording greater respect to the Pankhurst sisters or Martin Luther King. But some things also get worse. And of these the dewy-eyed Dawkins has scarcely anything to say. Nobody would gather from his smug account of the evolving wisdom of humanity that we are also faced with planetary devastation, the threat of nuclear conflict, the spreading catastrophe of AIDS and other deadly viruses, neoimperial zealotry, mass migrations of the dispossessed, political fanaticism, a reversion to Victorian-type economic inequalities, and a number of other potential catastrophes. For the champions of Progress, history is a cumulative tide of enlightenment laced with some minor currents of benightedness. A number of uncivilised anomalies wait to be sorted, mopped up, or ironed out. For Dawkins, the so-called War on Terror is no more than a historical hiccup. For the radical, by contrast, history is both civilisation and barbarism together. And the two are inseparably interwoven. Reading the likes of Dawkins, one realises why the doctrine of evil or original sin can be a radical kind of belief. It suggests that things are so dire with us that only a deep-seated transformation could hope to put them right.

Richard J. Bernstein writes in his book *Radical Evil* that the destruction of the World Trade Center in 2001 was "the very epitome of evil in our time."[12] He seems not to notice that the United States has killed inconceivably more innocent civilians in the past half century than the total number of those who perished in the tragedy in New York. As I write, perhaps several hundred times that number have been slaughtered in the criminal war in Iraq to which that tragedy gave birth. Bernstein passes over the tyrannies and butcheries perpetrated by his own nation in the name of liberty. Wickedness, it would seem, is always elsewhere. Today in the West, it is to be identified for the most part with those political regimes the United States cannot currently dominate, such as Iran and North Korea, as well as with Islamic terrorism, which indeed poses a grave (if much hyperbolised) threat to human well-being.

In the terms of this book, however, such terrorism is wicked rather than evil, and the distinction rests on far more than a verbal quibble. Indeed, our very security and survival may turn out to depend on it. The evil cannot be persuaded out of their destructive behaviour because there is no rationality behind what they do. For them, the rationality that other people seek to bring to bear on the issue is actually part of the problem. By contrast, it is theoretically possible to argue with those who use unscrupulous means to achieve rational or even admirable ends. The thirty-year conflict in Northern Ireland is over partly because armed Irish Republicanism fell squarely into this camp. But this might have been the case at one point with some Islamic fundamentalism too. Had the West acted differently in its treatment of certain Muslim nations, it might have escaped at least some of the aggression that is now being visited upon it.

This is not to claim that Islamic fundamentalism is eminently rational. On the contrary, it is ridden with the most virulent strains of prejudice and bigotry, as its torn and butchered victims have good reason to know. But those lethal fantasies are mixed in with some specific political grievances, however illusory or unjustified its enemies may consider them to be. To think otherwise is to imagine that Islamic terrorists, rather than being viciously wrong-headed, have no heads on their shoulders at all. It is to claim not that their grievances are misplaced, but that there is absolutely nothing to argue over. This is an irrational prejudice to rival their own, and one which can only make the situation worse. The tragedy is not only that millions of citizens now live in mortal danger through no fault of their own. It is also that such danger may never have been necessary in the first place.

No doubt there might still have been vicious, benighted Islamic ideologies around, just as there are vicious, benighted Western creeds. But it is unlikely that the twin towers would have crumbled simply because of this. It also took the Arab world's sense of anger and humiliation at the long history of its political abuse by the West. To define Islamic terrorism as evil, in the sense of the word employed in this book, is to refuse to recognise the reality of that wrath. It may well be too late for the kind of political action that might help to alleviate it. Terrorism now has a deadly momentum of its own. But there is a difference between regretting this tragically lost opportunity, and treating one's enemies as mindless beasts whom no rational action could ever conceivably sway. For champions of this viewpoint, the only solution to terrorist violence is more violence. More violence then breeds more terror, which in turn puts more blameless lives at risk. The result of defining terrorism as evil is to exacerbate the problem; and to make the problem worse is to be complicit, however unwittingly, in the very barbarism you condemn.

Notes

INTRODUCTION

1. See Fredric Jameson, *Fables of Aggression: Wyndham Lewis, the Modernist as Fascist* (Berkeley and London, 1979), p. 56.
2. See Perry Anderson, *The Origins of Postmodernity* (London, 1998), p. 65.

CHAPTER ONE
Fictions of Evil

1. Ewen Montagu, *The Man Who Never Was* (Stroud, 2007), p. ix.
2. Emmanuel Levinas, *Otherwise Than Being* (Pittsburgh, 1981), p. 192.
3. Theodor Adorno, *Negative Dialectics* (London, 1973), p. 156.
4. Herbert McCabe, *Faith Within Reason* (London, 2007), p. 160.
5. Terry Eagleton, *Jesus Christ: The Gospels* (London, 2007).
6. Richard J. Bernstein, *Radical Evil* (Cambridge, 2002), p. 229.
7. See Dermot Moran, *The Philosophy of John Scottus Eriugena* (Cambridge, 1989).
8. *Pseudo-Dionysus: The Complete Works* (New York, 1987), op. 98.
9. Slavoj Žižek, *Violence: Six Sideways Reflections* (London, 2008), p. 56.

10. Hannah Arendt, *Eichmann in Jerusalem: A Report on the Banality of Evil* (Harmondsworth, 1979), p. 288.
11. W. Kaufmann, ed., Friedrich Nietzsche, *On the Genealogy of Morals and Ecce Homo* (New York, 1979), p. 163.
12. Walter Benjamin, *Illuminations* (London, 1973), p. 244.
13. Søren Kierkegaard, *The Concept of Anxiety* (Princeton, NJ, 1980), p. 133.

CHAPTER TWO
Obscene Enjoyment

1. Terry Eagleton, *William Shakespeare* (Oxford, 1986), pp. 1–3.
2. R. L. Stevenson, *The Strange Case of Dr Jekyll and Mr Hyde* (London, 1956), p. 6.
3. Hannah Arendt, *Eichmann in Jerusalem: A Report on the Banality of Evil* (Harmondsworth, 1979), p. 54.
4. Ibid., p. 288.
5. Quoted in Peter Dews, *The Idea of Evil* (Oxford, 2007), p. 4.
6. Primo Levi, *The Drowned and the Saved* (London, 1988), p. 101.
7. Karl Jaspers, *Tragedy Is Not Enough* (London, 1934), p. 101.
8. Quoted by Peter Dews, *The Idea of Evil* (Oxford, 2007), p. 133.
9. Arthur Schopenhauer, *The World as Will and Idea* (New York, 1966), vol. 1, p. 364 (translation amended).
10. *The Confessions of St Augustine* (London, 1963), pp. 61–62.
11. Ibid., p. 72.
12. Søren Kierkegaard, *The Sickness unto Death* (London), p. 141.
13. Ibid., p. 48.
14. Ibid., pp. 48–49.
15. Ibid., p. 105.
16. See Terry Eagleton, *Holy Terror* (Oxford, 2005), p. 57.
17. *Henry James: Selected Literary Criticism* (Harmondsworth, 1963), p. 56.
18. For an excellent (if difficult) discussion of this problem, see

John Milbank, "Darkness and Silence: Evil and the Western Legacy," in *The Religious,* ed. John D. Caputo (Oxford, 2002).

19. Colin McGinn, *Ethics, Evil, and Fiction* (Oxford, 1997), p. 69f.

CHAPTER THREE
Job's Comforters

1. Kenneth Surin, *Theology and the Problem of Evil* (London, 1986), op. 32.
2. Richard Swinburne, *The Existence of God* (Oxford, 1979), p. 219.
3. Brian Davies, *The Reality of God and the Problem of Evil* (London and New York, 2006), p. 131.
4. Mary Midgley, *Wickedness: A Philosophical Essay* (London, 1984), p. 1.
5. Richard J. Bernstein, *Radical Evil* (Cambridge, 2002), p. 229.
6. Paul Ricoeur, *The Conflict of Interpretations* (Evanston, IN, 1974), p. 281.
7. Ibid., p. 3.
8. Arthur Schopenhauer, *The World as Will and Idea* (New York, 1969), vol. 2, p. 354.
9. Quoted by Peter Dews, *The Idea of Evil* (Oxford, 2007), p. 107.
10. Quoted in ibid., p. 124.
11. Richard Dawkins, *The God Delusion* (London, 2006), pp. 70–71.
12. Richard J. Bernstein, *Radical Evil* (Cambridge, 2002), p. x.

Index

Danton's Death (Buchner), 64
darkness, 127
Davies, Brian, 137
Dawkins, Richard, 155–56
death: being-toward death, 24;
   Christian theology on, 24; and
   corpse, 102; and despair, 114;
   and evil, 18; fear of, 26, 100; of
   God, 121; in Golding's *Pincher
   Martin,* 19–29, 52, 112; as joy,
   108; and love, 37; in Mann's
   Doctor Faustus, 70–71; of martyrs, 24; as non-being, 102;
   rehearsal of, in life, 24; stance
   toward, 70–71; two faces of,
   102. *See also* death drive
death drive: and death-in-life,
   114–16; and despair, 114–16;
   and destruction, 60–61, 127;
   and ecstatic sense of liberation, 108–9; and evil, 60–61,
   127; Freud on, 17–18, 60, 65,
   91, 98–99, 107–9, 112–13; and
   hell, 77–78; as imperishable,
   112–16; and melancholia, 110;
   and Nazism, 60, 112–13; in ordinary life, 128–29; and superego, 109. *See also* evil; nihilism
death-in-life, 114–16
debunkery, 87
demonic versus angelic state,
   74–76, 91–92, 101–2, 122–23
Denmark, 14–15
dependence, 12, 36

depression, 110
Derrida, Jacques, 47
desire, 113
despair, 78, 114–16
destruction: and evil, 60–62;
   and freedom, 33
determinism of character, 4–5
determinism of environment, 4
devil. *See* Satan
Dickens, Charles, 9–10, 120
difference and diversity, 39
Dionysian conception, 58–59
diversity and difference, 39
The Divine Names (Pseudo-
   Dionysus), 45
Doctor Faustus (Mann): as allegory of Nazi Germany, 60,
   64, 72; avant-garde music in,
   62–63, 66, 68–69, 71–74;
   death drive in, 59–60, 70–71,
   94–95; dissociation from
   body in, 81–82; evil as self-
   destruction in, 58–60, 63–64,
   94–95; freedom in, 33; hell in,
   67–68; humanist narrator's
   stance toward death in, 70;
   laughter of Leverkühn in, 76;
   Leverkühn as Dionysian artist
   in, 58–59; nihilism in, 66;
   rationalism of Leverkühn in,
   72–73; theological study by
   Leverkühn in, 54
Dostoevsky, Fyodor, 59, 117–19,
   133

dreams, 110
drinking. *See* alcoholism
drives, 35, 91. *See also* death drive

ego, 104, 108
egoism, 36, 107
Eichmann, Adolf, 51, 86–87, 123,
    129, 153
Eliot, T. S., 15, 57, 71
Emma (Austen), 19
Engels, Friedrich, 145
English Civil War, 132, 135
Enlightenment, 22–24, 132–33,
    136, 141
envy, 106, 129
Eriugena, John Scottus, 45–48, 67
Eros (life instincts), 60, 107–8
ethics, 14, 57
Ethics, Evil, and Fiction
    (McGinn), 105–6
Eve. *See* Adam and Eve
evil: angelic and demonic states
    of, 75–76, 101–2; as answer-
    able for one's own actions, 9;
    Aquinas on, 125; attempts at
    explanation and justification
    of, 131–43; Augustine on, 125–
    26; avant-garde art compared
    with, 62–63, 66, 68–69, 71–
    74; bad actions compared
    with, 107, 143; banality of,
    122–24; Barth on, 127–28;
    and Baudelaire's poetry, 122;
    Big Picture argument for, 138–
39; as body-spirit split, 21;
Boy Scout (or cold-shower)
case for, 133–34; and bureaucratic mind, 101; as conundrum or contradiction, 102–3;
as cosmic sulking, 117; and
cyclical time, 50; and death,
18; and death drive, 127; and
deficiency in art of living, 128;
denial of existence of, 16; and
destruction, 60–62; distinction between evil acts and evil
people, 151–53; and down-at-
heel heroism, 57; emptiness
and contentlessness of, 66;
and estrangement from creaturely existence, 57–58; everyday analogues of, 128–30;
features of, 49; as fixed ontological feature of human condition, 38; and freedom, 6–7,
30–31, 139–40; glamour of,
120–21; Gnostics on, 125; God
and existence of, 137–38; good
as result of, 134, 137–38; Hegel
on, 30–31, 147; and horror of
impurity, 102; and hostility
to material world, 47, 52;
immortality of, 50–51; Kant
on "radical" evil, 95; and lack
of know-how, 55; as lacking in
some vital dimension, 49; as
leeching life from others, 71;
and love of injustice, 94;

Manicheans on, 125–26; as metaphysical, 16, 66; as monotonous and boring, 49, 82–83, 123–24; motives causing wickedness and bad acts, 143–59; as mystery, 139; natural evil, 139; and nihilism, 13, 55–56, 68, 85, 87, 106, 118; and non-being and nothingness, 100–102, 128; as nostalgia for older, simpler civilization, 119–20; origin of, 63; as pointless, 84–85; positivity of, 127–28; "primitive" evil, 105–6; as projection, 107; public opinions on sin, 14–15; pure autonomy as dream of, 12; as pure disinterestedness, 93; as pure perversity, 94; as purposeless or nonpragmatic wickedness, 103–6; radicalism of, 120; rationality of, 103–4; and rejection of logic of causality, 84–85; resemblance between good and, 4, 9, 55, 66; and Satan of Milton's *Paradise Lost*, 6, 57, 62, 121; as Satanic possession, 3, 5–6; Schopenhauer on, 107; as self-dependent, 63; self-thwarting nature of, 117–18; slime associated with, 82–83; social systems and wickedness, 144–48, 151; superficial nature of, 49;

as timeless condition, 53; as transcendence, 55, 65; as transitional state, 123–24; as uncaused or its own cause, 3–4; as unintelligible, 2–3, 8; unreality of, 49; virtue versus, 120. *See also* death drive; and specific authors and titles

The Exorcist, 5–6

Falklands war, 133
farce, 87
fascism, 60, 69–70, 72, 95–96. *See also* Nazism
Faust (Goethe), 26, 61, 65
Faustian Man, 31, 113
Fenianism, 3
fetishes, 91, 100, 110
feudalism, 136–37
Fielding, Henry, 19
Finnegans Wake (Joyce), 50
forgiveness, 40–41, 56, 110
fortunate Fall, 30, 135–37
Francis of Assisi, Saint, 150
Free Fall (Golding), 30–31, 34–35, 39–41
freedom: and destructiveness, 33; and evil, 6–7, 30–31, 139–40; of God, 46, 140; and hell, 24–25, 54–55; and original sin, 33; and reason, 7; and self-destruction, 63–64; and social influences, 9, 11–12
Freud, Sigmund: on death drive,

Freud (*continued*)
17–18, 60, 65, 91, 98–99, 107–
9, 112–13; on desire, 33; on
dreams, 110; on drives, 91; on
fetish, 91; on love as bound up
with resentment and aggression, 34; on melancholia, 110;
on obscene enjoyment, 75; on
psychopathological features of
everyday life, 129–30; on sublimation, 91; on superego, 1,
109; on unconscious, 46, 70,
91, 110
fundamentalism, 74, 100, 119,
121, 122, 157–58

gay people, 39, 99
Genet, Jean, 69
Gide, André, 97
Gnosticism, 125
God: Aquinas on, 45, 125;
Augustine on, 64–65; as black
lightning in Golding's *Pincher
Martin,* 25–28; as cause of
himself, 4; creation by, 61–62,
63, 140; death of, 121; Enlightenment view of, 141; Eriugena
on, 45–46, 67; and existence
of evil, 137–38; freedom of,
46, 140; and laws of logic,
126–27; love and mercy of,
24–28, 54, 55; of Milton's *Paradise Lost,* 120; mystery of,
141–42; as non-being, 45–46,
67; as own reason for being,
84; perfection of, 125; Pseudo-
Dionysus on, 45; rejection of,
24–25, 54–55, 64–65, 120; and
theodicy, 132–43
The God Delusion (Dawkins),
155–56
Goebbels, Joseph, 11
Goethe, Johann Wolfgang von,
61, 65
Golding, William: *Free Fall* by,
30–31, 34–35, 39–41; *The
Inheritors* by, 29–30; *Lord of
the Flies* by, 1–2, 29, 37. *See
also Pincher Martin* (Golding)
goodness: and acceptance of evil
by embracing it in love and
mercy, 56; as answerable for
one's own actions, 9; Aquinas
on, 61, 124–25; Blake on, 125;
complex practical skills of, 36;
distinction between good acts
and good people, 151–52; evil
versus, 120; as free of social
conditioning, 9; in Greene's
Brighton Rock, 55, 56, 58; of
human nature, 128–29, 147–
49; and immortality, 50; and
lack of know-how, 55; and love
of unfinished nature of things,
101; and materialism, 150–51;
as metaphysical, 66; middle
class and virtue, 120; and perfection of thing in itself, 124–

25, 140–41; in private versus public domain, 147; puritan view of virtue, 10; resemblance between evil and, 4, 9, 55, 66; as result of evil, 134, 137–38; Schopenhauer on, 106–7; as transcendence, 55

grace, 114

Green, André, 103

Greene, Graham, 51–58, 61, 68, 94, 103, 114, 119, 124

guilt, 34–35, 40, 109–10

Hamlet (Shakespeare), 108

happiness, 17, 146–47

Hardy, Thomas, 34, 155

heaven, 134

Hegel, G. W. F., 14, 30–31, 114, 146–47

hell: of alcoholic, 115; as beyond language, 67; as boring, 124; and death drive, 77–78; desolation and despair of, 78; devil on, 76–77; as eternal monotony of oneself, 22; extinction in, 25; fear of, 25; finality of, 25; fires of, 117–18; and freedom, 24–25, 54–55; Lacan on, as *Ate*, 78; masochists in, 77–78; and nihilism, 78; O'Brien's *The Third Policeman* as allegory of, 41–51, 95; and rejection of God, 24–25, 54–55; Sartre on, 22; uncanniness of, 49

history, 146–47, 154–55

Hitler, Adolf, 7, 51, 64, 97, 99, 152, 153. *See also* Nazism

"Hollow Men" (Eliot), 57

Holmes, Sherlock, 3

Holocaust, 18, 65, 87, 96–102, 112–13, 127, 134, 142, 152–53. *See also* Nazism

homosexuals. *See* gay people

human nature, 46, 128–29, 147–49, 153–56. *See also* body

humanism, 16, 145

Hume, David, 128–29

Iago. *See Othello* (Shakespeare)

id, 108

idealism, 75, 88–92, 102

identity, 103–4

ideology, 145

illness, 38, 134, 139

Immaculate Conception, 35

immortality, 50–51

impurity, 97–102

infants. *See* children

The Inheritors (Golding), 29–30

Inquisition, 98

Iran, 157

Iraq war, 157

Ireland. *See* Northern Ireland

Irish Fenianism, 3

Irish Republican Army, 8–9

Islamic fundamentalism, 121, 157–58

Islamic terrorism, 7–8, 156–59

mass psychosis, 96–97
materialism, 150–53
mathematics, 67
Mathers, Cotton, 45
McCabe, Herbert, 36
McFarlane, John, 29
McGinn, Colin, 105–6, 129
melancholia, 110
Mensheviks, 136
The Merchant of Venice (Shakespeare), 85
middle class: mediocrity of, 68; and moralism, 14, 56–57, 69, 120; pure autonomy as dream of, 12
Midgley, Mary, 141–43
The Midwich Cuckoos (Wyndham), 2
Milton, John, 6, 57, 62, 120, 121, 132, 135–37
modernism, 70–72
Montagu, Ewen, 28–29
Moral Majority, U.S., 14
moralism, 14, 56–57, 68–69, 150
mourning, 37
murder: of children, 1, 3–7, 9, 12–13, 96; as divine power, 120; by Stalin and Mao, 96, 97, 127, 145
music. *See* avant-garde music
Muslims. *See* Islamic terrorism

natural disasters, 131, 133–34, 139
Nature, 52, 72, 98, 135, 139

Nazism: and abnegation of freedom, 63; compared with Stalin and Mao, 97; and death camps, 96–97, 99, 127, 142; and dual face of evil, 75, 101–2; and Eichmann, 86–87, 123, 129, 152–53; and fundamentalism, 100; in Golding's *Free Fall*, 41; and hatred of material reality, 47, 75, 101–2; and Hitler, 7, 51, 64, 97, 99, 152, 153; and Holocaust, 18, 65, 87, 96–102, 112–13, 127, 134, 142, 152–53; and idealism, 75, 102; and Jews as ontological threat, 99–102; as modernist phenomenon, 72; and non-being and nothingness, 100–102; and Other, 99–101; and pathological drive to self-identity, 104; and purification of the race, 97–99; rallies of, 124; and self-destruction, 60; and SS, 16; and suburban morality, 69
New Age, 122
Nietzsche, Friedrich, 47, 52, 72, 115, 139
nihilism: and angelic societies, 123; and evil, 13, 55–56, 68, 85, 87, 106, 118; and hell, 78; in Mann's *Doctor Faustus*, 60, 66; and negativity, 155; and Nietzsche, 52. *See also* death drive

North Korea, 95, 157
Northern Ireland, 14–15, 157
Norwich, John Julius, 29
nothingness, 100–102, 115, 127.
 See also nihilism
nuclear conflict, 156

O'Brien, Flann, 41–51, 95, 124,
 127
obscene enjoyment, 75–78, 100–
 101, 111–12
Oliver Twist (Dickens), 9–10
Operation Mincemeat, 28–29
original sin, 29–37, 39–41, 110,
 126, 148, 151
Orwell, George, 29
Othello (Shakespeare), 25, 85–92,
 93, 99, 104, 110
Other, 99–101

Pankhurst sisters, 156
Paradise Lost (Milton), 6, 57, 62,
 120, 121, 132, 135–36
Paul, Saint, 56, 110, 114
Philosophical Investigations
 (Wittgenstein), 68, 105
Pincher Martin (Golding): black
 lightning in, 25–28, 53–54;
 brutal self-interest in, 20–24;
 "dark centre" of Pincher Martin in, 22–24; death in, 19–
 29, 52, 112; dissociation from
 body in, 21, 81–82; dissolution
 of rock, sky, and ocean at end

of, 27–28, 48, 91; evil as purposeless or nonpragmatic
 wickedness in, 103; as fable of
 purgatory, 24, 41; fear of nothingness in, 115; hell as vacuity
 in, 67; illusion of Pincher
 Martin in, 78; ruthless self-
 interest in, 93–94
pleasure principle, 109
postmodernism, 15, 38–39, 99,
 121–22
pride, 26, 60, 117, 118
progressivism, 155–56
projection, 107
Prometheus, 23
Proverbs of Heaven and Hell
 (Blake), 125
Pseudo-Dionysus, 45
psychoanalysis, 17–18, 35, 91, 105,
 107–8, 113, 127. See also Freud,
 Sigmund
purgatory, 24, 41
purification of the race, 97–99
puritanism, 10, 31, 120

radical evil, 95, 156–57
Radical Evil (Bernstein), 156–57
radicals and revolutionaries, 118–
 19, 148–50
Rawls, John, 94
reality principle, 109
reason: and body, 32–33; and
 evil, 132–33; and freedom, 7;
 as meaning void of life, 73

religious fundamentalism, 74,
100, 119, 121, 122, 157–58
responsibility, 10–12
revolutionaries and radicals, 118–
19, 149–50
Richard III (Shakespeare), 6
Ricoeur, Paul, 143
Rimbaud, Arthur, 68
Roman Catholicism, 35, 126. *See
also* Christianity
Romans, Epistle to, 110
Rousseau, Jean-Jacques, 36
Russian Bolsheviks, 149
Russian Mensheviks, 136

Sade, Marquis de, 93
sadism, 105–6, 128, 152
saints, 56–57, 68–69
Sartre, Jean-Paul, 6, 22, 63, 93
Satan: as angel and demon, 75;
as author of nothing, 62; in
Dostoevsky's *The Brothers
Karamazov,* 133; as fallen
angel, 63; on hell, 76–77;
laughter of, 74; in Mann's
Doctor Faustus, 68, 76–77; of
Milton's *Paradise Lost,* 6, 57,
62, 121; pride of, 26, 60; reactionary nature of, 119–20; as
supercilious intellectual and
vulgar clown, 73–74
Satanic possession, 3, 5–6
Satanism, 59, 122
Saved (Bond), 12

scapegoat, 35, 56
Schadenfreude (malicious delight
in others' misfortunes), 128
Schelling, F. W. J., 47
Schoenberg, Arnold, 68
Schopenhauer, Arthur, 61, 106–
7, 112, 135, 146, 147, 155
The Secret Scripture (Barry), 62
self-destruction, 63–64, 88, 94–
95. *See also* death drive; suicide
self-determination, 12
Sex and Character (Weininger),
100
sexuality, 52, 53, 122, 126, 152
Shakespeare, William: *Coriolanus* by, 86; Fool of, 81; *Hamlet* by, 108; *Macbeth* by, 79–85,
86, 89, 90, 95, 103; *The Merchant of Venice* by, 85; *Othello*
by, 25, 85–92, 93, 99, 104, 110;
Richard III by, 6; *The Tempest*
by, 81; villains of, 12; *The Winter's Tale* by, 90–91
sin: Augustine on pleasure of,
111; belief in, 14–15; God's love
for sinners, 55, 68–69; original sin, 29–37, 39–41, 110,
126, 148, 151; Paul on, 110; of
pride, 26, 60. *See also* evil
slavery, 136
social influences, 9, 11–12
socialism, 69–70, 136–37, 148–50
Soviet Union, 11, 149. *See also*
Stalin, Joseph

Stalin, Joseph, 96, 97, 145
Sterne, Laurence, 42
Stevenson, Robert Louis, 82, 123
The Strange Case of Dr. Jekyll and Mr. Hyde (Stevenson), 82, 123
sublimation, 91
suffering, 106, 107, 134–35, 138, 142
suicide, 63–64, 88, 94–95, 110
superego, 1, 108, 109–10
Surin, Kenneth, 132
Swinburne, Richard, 133–34

The Tempest (Shakespeare), 81
terrorism, 5, 7–8, 156–59
Thanatos. See death drive
theodicy, 132–43
The Third Policeman (O'Brien), 41–51, 95, 124, 127
Tom Jones (Fielding), 19
transcendence, 122–23
transgression, 121–22
Treatise of Human Nature (Hume), 128–29
Tristram Shandy (Sterne), 42

Ulysses (Joyce), 34
unconscious, 46, 70, 91, 110
Under the Volcano (Lowry), 115

vampire, 71, 122, 123
violence. *See* Nazism; terrorism
virtue. *See* goodness
viruses, 140–41, 156

Waiting for Godot (Beckett), 50
The Waste Land (Eliot), 71
Weininger, Otto, 100
wickedness. *See* bad actions; evil
Wilde, Oscar, 34
Will, 107, 112
The Winter's Tale (Shakespeare), 90–91
witches, 79–85, 90, 95, 103
Wittgenstein, Ludwig, 68, 105
women, 100
Women in Love (Lawrence), 72–73, 118–19
The World as Will and Idea (Schopenhauer), 106–7
World War I, 8
World War II, 28–29
Wyndham, John, 2

Yeats, W. B., 50, 59, 70

Žižek, Slavoj, 50–51